Falling in Love Falling in Love With You Syntax: Selected and New Poems

Published Books

A Clove of Gender.
Stride Press, U.K. 1995. 158 pp.

Pure Mental Breath.
Gesture Press, Toronto, Ontario, Canada. 1994. 81 pp.

Tommy and Neil.
Sun/Gemini Press, Tucson, Arizona. 1993. 90 pp.

Teth.
Chax Press, Tucson, Arizona. 1991. 91 pp.

Sad Isn't the Color of the Dream.
Stride Press, U.K. 1991. 100 pp.

With House Silence.
Stride Press, U.K. 1987. 64 pp.

Chapbooks

A Little Syncopy.
Marshall Creek Press, P.O. Box 305, Ben Lomond, CA 95005. 1996. 28 pp.

Three Works in Way #2.
Edited by Tom Beckett.
131 North Pearl Street. Kent, Ohio. 44240. 1996. 32 pp.

Since We Last Met.
Raunchland Publications, Transition Series Number 6. Scotland. 1996. 10 pp.

Between Pipelines
NinthLab Electronic Chaps. 1996. 8 pp.

The Ghost of Parmenides (with John M. Bennett).
Anabasis Electronic Chaps. 1996. 18 pp.

Virgule.
Burning Llama Press, 1995. 24 pp.

Wind Topography.
Standing Stones Press, 1992. 11 pp.

Thoughtsongs.
Tin Wreath Press, 1992. 6 pp.

Literal Ponds.
Potes & Poets Press, 1992. 20 pp.

The Dessert Cart of Synecdoche.
Trombone Press, U.K. 1992. 20 pp.

18/81.
(excerpt from the book Pure Mental Breath, prior to publication by Gesture Press, Canada). 1991. 24 pp.

Criteria for Being Touched.
Experimental Press, Tucson, Arizona. 1991. 6 pp.

A Rich Timetable and Appendices.
Luna Bisonte Prods Press, Columbus, Ohio. 1991. 12 pp.

Obeli: 21 Contemplations.
Pygmy Forest Press. Albion, California. 1990. 21 pp.

Lens Rolled in a Heart.
(collaboration with John M. Bennett) Etymon Press, Australia. 1991. 15 pp.

Loss Prevention Photograph, Some Pencils and a Memory Elastic.
Tape Books, Scotland. 1988. 36 pp.

The Truth Right Now.
Bakhtin's Wife Publications. San Diego, California. 1988. 30 pp.

This Stem Much Stronger Than Your Spine.
M.A.F. Press. Portlandville, New York. 1987. 28 pp.

Memory Transposed into the Key of C.
Mockersatz Press. Sterling, Virginia, 1986. 8 pp.

Appropriate Behavior.
Abbey Press. Columbia, Maryland, 1986. 13 pp.

Late Summer.
Pierian Press, Canada. 1984. 12 pp.

Virtuoso Bird.
Brushfire Press, Phoenix, Arizona. 1981. 24 pp.

Falling in Love Falling in Love With You Syntax: Selected and New Poems

by

Sheila E. Murphy

Potes & Poets Press, Inc.
Elmwood, CT 1997

Potes & Poets Press, Inc
181 Edgemont Avenue
Elmwood, CT 06110-1005, U.S.A.
email: potepoet@home.com

FIRST EDITION
Copyright © Shelia E. Murphy, 1997
All rights reserved

ISBN 0-937013-66-8
Printed in the United States of America

Writer's Statement

This work documents a part of living that takes place in decibels. Again, again, its pulse points locate frequencies to carry them. Now seasoned with successive hearings, members of the tone row sound themselves to me. Pressing harmonic places as companion nerves from womb time with a mother who conducted. In a spaced geometry grown useful, standard, woven, blue, or mezzo. Where flute repeats its reputation, free to vary.

I live the discipline I'm constantly inventing to afford a state of heart with mind not previously known. Priming the antennae has become my major practice. In the hope of raising probability that music will be found translatable to languages still being learned. That syllables in patterns form new instruments with body and with tact.

The cornucopia resists dismantling, entrusts its shape to expectations seeded in thought process rumored to be random. The color wheel within tonality unbuttons conscience nearing a profusion of discovery. A kinaesthetic atmosphere delineates new coats of paint that signal one vibration and a next. Heuristics unlace tension or promote it till we swerve apart from weather.

Biography cohabits with experiment. I relax into a light that echoes incubator where lore has it I replied with closure of these noticeable eyes. Now I listen and engage the hand with inexpensive ballpoints and a keyboard to release vocabulary onto screens, in search of fluency.

Writing is itself experience, not mere transcription or a washed event refashioned in unlikely solitude. I am sure no poem could have been found or made at any different time or place from when and where it gelled. So I stay awake for it, alert to the arrival while living the concurrencies. Primed for making, I revel in the luxury of spawning code immune to a deciphering.

This volume includes work from six previously published full-length collections, spanning the mid-1980s to approximately 1994. Each has its own identity apart from mine. I am grateful to Rupert Loydell of Stride Press; Charles Alexander of Chax Press; Clint Colby of SUN/gemini Press; and Nick Power of Gesture Press for making those books available. Also included here are several new poems that have appeared in the following periodicals, whose publishers I also thank: *Phoebe, Grist-on-Line, Ribot, Big Scream, Kiosk, First Intensity, Lost* and *Found Times, Intuit, Dirigible, The Alterran Poetry Assemblage,* and *Dadababy.*

Sheila E. Murphy
February 18, 1997

for my mother, Bernadean Flynn Murphy

Approximate Quotation

How music comes into your life when, say, you're destroyed is the subject of the first poem in this book. In it, distraught, she becomes the house and then by way of the flute becomes the world again. This is what we'd call the "subject" of a poem in prose like Baudelaire's. Her words are French, "resign," bourgeois." Yet if you look at Baudelaire's *Petits Poemes* you'll see that how he gets from word to word is all of it for him, baritone to trill, "arpeggiated softness." So here, a sentence could be lifted out, it's true, but it matters that it's just *here*. Gertrude Stein's word for that is "composition." No sentence, in Sheila, is a simple declarative. Her sentences, even driven by memory as in *Tommy and Neil*, are neighborhoods. What she does *with* house silence is "tamper." Music in that poem brings the world back. The world is "Found," first word in the sentence (the "I" is silent.) Nobody else would follow, there, birds and laughter with "aimless humming." All this from a flute, cold in blue velvet? Certainly not. The poem is about healing, and what it says is that healing is experienced as a composition. The music doesn't produce a world, like the masque in *Tempest*. "If birds sang, I did not know them," modulates to card catalogue "no longer" including composers, no more knowable than the birds. But the poem, a composition, includes with a light touch the act of writing itself. I said "including composers" from the license of approximate quotation. Sheila wrote "included," a lumpishly trilled "d," included composers, no longer included composers, It grew so quiet I thought the card catalogue no longer included composers, the sentence itself picking up the "not" after If birds sang, and as I said repeating, expanding birds not known into composers once familiar now not known, even as objects of research (though at best known only as such, not played, not heard), and unavailable to any concourse of scholars, not just Sheila. When her world goes, ours went, the disability global. As she writes these lines writing, as well as music, becomes a sign of health. She composes about a composition that is about, and is, composing oneself.

When in "WFMT Haibun" she writes about strain (neatly contained in *Stravin*sky) the verbs and adverbs get a little strained, just a little. As you go on reading these in sequence, perhaps like a Bach exercise book, you'll find her metaphors begin to take over whole sentences. The sentences pull farther apart from each other as they get more self-involved, the care as if to do a passage, each sentence a passage. Subjects become implicit, ghost-subjects. Yet the whole is still a composition, pulled back to itself in those isolated last-line triple finishes. The visual isolation (not even a period) is density, increased *overall* precision, collapsar.

So these are bravery and performance, in a way, and that's why so much childhood uncertainty, reprised, gets into these, the unsettlingness of life, how a light switch can be self-doubt. "The Physical," a convalescent poem, informs you in a complete sentence "As I aspire to give the bones and muscles relaxation from what has not happened yet." The insight, recognizable to us, is a complete sentence because incomplete. The writing is nonchalant, recognizing in one mode what it knows in another (you'd say), but *I* never noticed that prospective relaxation till Sheila wrote it. Takes me back to mornings on circuses, the day to come. Very early the writing, a long stretch of years now, becomes a device for noticing things, open to its own disconcertion. These sentences are not different to be different, except sometimes with the patient malice of children playing with excised clockwork. The percentage of really good two-word phrases goes up.

The more hermetic she gets, the more personal. Words can't "aspire" (horrible word) to the condition of music but her really hard ones, where she blows most free to render some state for which there's never been a word, pull half-recognitions out of you the way music can. I like the alternation of these, in this book, with the straightforward essay-poems, linear even if each sentence is bent by a perceived metaphor (which is why her nouns in these feel like verbs), bound to an argument, her business letters, available because the job she gives herself is like jobs we give ourselves. But the world's invited in more in her hardest ones.

In this she is like Baudelaire, Mallarmé, conventions and a reader's expectations just material, the tendency of crystals to make *some* pattern on a window a thing to play against, deeply social when most obscure. We don't, in English, know so well how to be social when difficult, take obscurity as a pulling away (or worse, a pulling in). This wouldn't be worth mentioning only Sheila deserves being read by people who are not professional audiences for poetry. I can hear them say "This doesn't make sense." Well, "The Raven" doesn't make sense. At no point does "The Raven" make sense. It may look it, but no poem is less than what it's about. The Symbolist poet presented a face like Pierrot's, unreal, and people picked that up. Sheila's difficulty is not a false face because it is not a face. Ellipsis is an eyebrow, as Poe's clarity is an expression of the eyes above a poem, saying it. And so on, badly, because we imagine communication as a gist or burden, reducible to newspaper English. "I write like a sieve accepting rinse travelling through lightspeed. Retain only the moisture then the thought of flow." This is clear the way Poe is clear, unexpectedly clear, even unacceptably clear, and you find "The crevices between equally musical." Her brothers xylophones and saxophones. *Any* model of translation belies her "nounliness of form that genuflects to content." I did that wrong by quoting her as if to be clear, presenting her phrase as if a summation like a wisecrack. She likes words like "practicum." You don't interrogate a liking that animal. "Pausing to take breath and become it." Her sentences are traps for writers of prefaces. The habit is now to excise one, then another, call it criticism. I call it shopping.

The title-poem of this collection would translate well, is made out of sentences that are the raw material of which translations are made. French, Spanish. Imagine Cisneros, or little Clarice Lispector, reading these, some local newspaper gritty gray, provincial, their hearts moved perfectly well by the sequence of these sentences in sequence. Her wit is often serial, a quality I seem to find more in women than in men, that if so transcends languages. The "J" letters she's been writing lately seem to be untranslatable. Maybe Portuguese. I've trouble with her memory as scrapbook, letters to her brothers uninvolved at the theoretical level with the recognizable, the shared. They say relations with your family are not what the French would call a problematic. It's true as assertion, but anything you assert is true, so I pick up at poems like "Informal Logic," which renders memory as selection among seepage, the way that if you could render it (as Sheila does) could get you put away. Poems you read like entrails. It is, right now, how I read Poe, or Dylan Thomas, a vatic reading. Quite long stretches of poems here do not do that. Quite long stretches do.

Gerald Burns

Title/First Words	Page

from With House Silence

With House Silence	3
WFMT Haibun	4
Retracing	5
Daily Bread	6
Fanatacism	7
For Seeing Greater Distances	8
Entry Level	9
The Physical	10
Self Spiralling	11
Plain Old Thursday	12
Tradition	13
A Saxophone Wind Presses	14
Biography	15
A Tentative	16
Visualization	17
Cheesecloth: Spiritual	18
Sacrifice	19
Haibun 16	20

from Sad Isn't the Color of the Dream

I'm Best at Playing the Game When	
I'm Not Playing the Game	23
A Portrait of Beverly C	24
Sunflower	25
Some Yellows, Some Dark Blues, a Chocolate Color	26
Where She Is Living Now	27
The Question Following the Statement	28
Pressure	29
Aspirations	30
A Portrait: Norm	31
Sad Isn't the Color of the Dream	32
Use of the Generic Masculine	33
Overdue Books	34
Portrait: Eleven Years	35

Title/First Words	Page
Portrait of the Other	37
Joy	39
Meditation on Impatience	40
Mass at the Crypt	41
Falling in Love Falling in Love with You Syntax	42

from Teth

"insinuate a dream..."	45
"virgin prophet indigo..."	46
"refrigerator transforms..."	47
"borscht akimbo during vodka..."	48
"mahatma fox I call her..."	49
"long distance breastmilk..."	50
"per our agreement thistling..."	51
"tome is wisecrack..."	52
"is she radiant..."	53
"learn the womb can't..."	54
"gendarmes inside remember..."	55
"maybe we project..."	56
"preambular morning..."	57
"yacht floats..."	58
"casual with words..."	59
"logic mostly snatches birds..."	60
"hysterical post-rain mockingbirds..."	61
"virtually pinned to incapacity..."	62
"accept then weave the center..."	63
"ideogram..."	64
"indebtedness tips guilt..."	65
"trousers and holster with tools..."	66
"inspires regret..."	67
"digital clockface..."	68

Title/First Words	Page

from **Tommy and Neil**

first section: Tommy

"Playpen caged your beauty."	71
"Touched his head."	72
"Cherry trees were tall."	73
"What does water soothe?"	74
"Mother's potato salad..."	75
"You watched him..."	76
"*Tosca* might have been..."	77
"Tears want to be..."	78
"My conscience takes you..."	79
"You reflexively seem able..."	80
"Bluish wood along..."	81
"Having preceded your world..."	82
"I write from a proximity..."	83
"Choice I'm always not touching..."	84

second section: Letters to Neil

"Before you could speak..."	87
"Thematic whine..."	88
"We worry as a pair."	89
"You invited Jimmy Carter..."	90
"Members of the John Adams..."	91
"You would dance inside..."	92
"People use your name..."	93
"Dad would discuss stocks..."	94
"You empty the hot pipe..."	95
"Twelve years ago..."	96
"I like you and your handshake..."	97
"Was I an event you watched..."	98
"You prepare somebody lateral..."	99
"How do you work..."	100
"You stood on Central Avenue..."	101

Title/First Words	Page

from Pure Mental Breath

"Blossom, synonymous with curfew..."	105
"Balcony, the sea, a wave..."	106
"Parentheses keep us warm..."	107
"Road becomes so instantly..."	108
"Compose a white chenille..."	109
"Tender knows the power..."	110
"Amiable mention seabreeze..."	111
"Strawberry tenders resignation..."	112
"Croquet is being symptomatic..."	113
"Substance missing from charisma..."	114
"Rain isn't what I like..."	115
"Surprise is chariot..."	116
"Breath moves sacred..."	117
"Legend pores over itself..."	118
"Percussion is without..."	119
"Clarity mimes truth..."	120
"Neighborhood extends the reach..."	121
"Self economizes..."	122

from A Clove of Gender

from Section I. The Weight and Feel of Harps

The Weight and Feel of Harps	125
Would Be a Father Noiselessly	126
The Lullaby of Sun	127
Beautiful Sunwarm Arizona...	128

from Section II. Informal Logic

A Pint of Training Wheels	133
Informal Logic	134

from Section III. Desert Wildflowers

Desert Hibiscus	137

Title/First Words	Page
Coulter Hibiscus	138
Spring Evening Primrose	139
Engelmann Prickly Pear	140
Desert Mariposa	141
Fremont Pincushion	142

from Section IV. Literal Ponds

"literal ponds..."	145
"trace (by hand..."	146
"disposable appearing flowers..."	147
"literature fathoms..."	148
"'train paintings to lie still...'"	149
"romance glistens comparable..."	150
"the Sunday roast..."	151
"*nothing*, rich and ripe..."	152

from Section V. How Partial Therefore Lovel

This Margin	155
Weather Business	156
Each Other's Line of Breath	157
Eros	158
When Clouds, Class Clown	159

from Section VI. For Leisure, Boundaries

"Come Harvard me..."	163
"for leisure, boundaries..."	164
"pallor, chipt paint..."	165
"what about her ego..."	166

from Section VII. Wind Topography

"I'm talking in your sleep..."	169
"a lexicon abbreviating..."	170
"connectedly we sing..."	171
"expertise seems floundering..."	172

Title/First Words	Page

New Poems: Previously Uncollected

Gorecki in July	175
Thales	177
She's Lovely on Prozac	178
Iff	179
Remarkable Attention	192
Isosceles Relationships	193
A Mood Apart from Singing Charles Ives	194
Wild Yam	195
The Tonsure Cure (Lui-Meme)	196
Abscondily with Plenty Mercredi	197
Frame	198
Dividends	199
Subjects	200
We Would Be Sheep	201

Interview with Sheila E. Murphy

Interview	204

from

With House Silence

With House Silence

Then music got up and walked out of my life. I didn't hear it tiptoeing away. My hands and feet numb, I sat moving paper almost silently from a tall pile onto a shorter one. The world seemed the world, was all. I didn't hear it resign, only the paychecks stopped. Free time, nothing to buy. I thought the monovoice of every neighbor a smear of carbon left on white soap cake. Stopped reading newspapers to keep clean. Shoved the windows closed. If birds sang, I did not know them. It grew so quiet I thought the card catalogue no longer included composers. My composition was "adapt." I became the color of walls, then curtains. One day when coal burned warmth back into me, I reached for the dry sketches I had performed above the calendar. And saw that I was 33 years old. The flute cold in blue velvet, inside leather case. And shyly tampered with house silence. Found birds, laughter, aimless humming. Underpinnings, arpeggiated softness. Perfect hearing.

Coolness, rehearsal a return, first new song

WFMT Haibun

Stravinsky nervous woodwinds arm wrestle with percussive slits of piano castanets and bassly the various brass stretch their necks to notice what is going on. Then the sledge corrodes some driveway bravely as the world attempts to squeeze through, a slum kid pressing 300 to pass freshman year. Some of the harmony rasping solipsistically negates the he-man prospects of an early evening. Muted brass and someone wearing thick soled rubber thongs slogs through a rainfall dissonantly if alone that could be possible.

Not what you get only, also what you give, exclusive of equilibrium

Retracing

It goes all of a sudden white. Desire matches a printout of my loneliness. This soft shirt run through multiple washes confronting only water. I think all sorts of things about your photograph. What we could become. But I don't say them, for the unreachable remains a beacon. Everything transformed in its light. In the eyes of those wanting. Almost 1:30 in the morning propped up in my bed I simulate the drinking days with seltzer water, about as good as beer minus the intrigue. Maybe take it from the bottle straight. People like me should not live alone. Notice we never do. Tomorrow in late afternoon I'll cook for friends. They will love the talk and make a thing to share.

Leather puzzle, acupuncture, reminisce a color momentarily

Daily Bread

Fundraising for my heart. Blood pressure pressuring my nervous system with data littering the earth like dotted swiss amoeba. Pets of pets in breathless cell blocks. Choreography accommodating light gauze. Air handlers with tiny hearing aids penetrate breezeways. Hypertension rides its bicycle up my street. I poke stop signs into several lawns. Copiously note pantries needing respirators for insects. Dream collective nouns. Occasional blank inquiries decomposing before thought. Almost able to speak perfectly. What was noticed, vegetable oil on otherwise white screen. Hand shadows as commercial messages within live narrative.

Oath of office, preamble, narcissism

Fanaticism

Windows poked from tenements. I wonder where the stick is now that shattered all the second story glass into thick cobwebs, maybe broke them, too. Political act allowing my attention span to focus on pointillist inkling of anarchy. Mirror signal channeling sunlight to say danger if we can only read the signal properly. No need to describe the house. It is every dwelling we have slept in dreaming incorrigible madness wanting to leap from ourselves like cherry bombs fired into a crowd of only children.

Needle in haystack, matchbook, purity, charred fingers

For Seeing Greater Distances

Philosophy is the treehouse we continually wind up playing in. I like its demure smile, every little fleck of eyebrow pencil noise that interferes with duty and accompanying reality. The telescope propped in a corner reminds me I am eligible for seeing greater distances. But cozy is seductive, primping the particulars within its four walls, the equivalent of compass points, springboards for departure in the direction of unknown winds. I harbor insecurity and greed. Warring impulses inviting immobility or speed truncating the natural flow of verbs inaugurating pressure I induce myself.

Rest area, birthing idea and the practical intrusion, clock and calendar

Entry Level

A chore to laminate relationships with don't-touch-me transparent plastic coating. Leave something for your diary so a stranger can enter the sheets like a cricket sliding through a hole to the left of the front door, too small for the thumb. Violation contains ambivalence. Glad for the company, infuriated at being disturbed. Say I love you to the beast who's broken down your home, be a fairy tale for someone's comfort.

Scrapbook positioned outside nature, dust between young fingers

The Physical

I love the chair with gelding passion. Pleased that it faces the precise color TV, allowing the world into my mind if I'm unable to effect its transformation. An underspin skillfully executed in a match. From my chair I watch nothing able to challenge me. As I aspire to give the bones and muscles relaxation from what has not happened yet. Training the engine in the art of genuflection to the body that must carry out assignments of intelligence.

Escape, an ammunition pungent in tabled amnesty

Self Spiralling

Some dignitaries I wanted to worry about knowing have made it easy for me to become them. I keep a straight face, hoping to elude their suspicion of my trying to absorb practices that help reclassify me. Evolution is related to a flushing of old mirrors from the system, removal of plate glass embedded like nerve fibers in the skin. As others have perceived me I perceive myself. This new image, unrelated to a precedent, dissolves. I ponder the mystique which now surrounds me. Having attributed this foggy honor to importances that I could not possess.

Faith healing, maybe the suppression of old photo albums

Plain Old Thursday

After a lot of dithering around with fame and visibility, it's nice to know that plain old Thursday has reserved a space for you in one of its lean rows. Your powdery wings prefer a rest from the exhaustion. It's so quiet far away from imaginary life on this lip of weekend with new movies to anoint king of the collective consciousness. You try whistling behind your closed office door. Looking out the window for a long time to organize your thoughts about various aspects of the hem haw cluttered universe. Loose coins in denominations much too small to notice. Daytime has this feature you would willingly enjoy, with proper direction. But no one anywhere seems willing to divulge the secret *some*body must be aware of. Maybe the pope or priests, on the occasion of Holy Orders. But such large questions are fit only for tremendous minds in their exalted moments. For now, it's only Thursday, thank God, not your inauguration or even anybody's birthday.

Commonplace event, release, a twitching that tweaks itself awake, less artificially alive

Tradition

Stale piano yields gems pianissimo. Notes joined by pedal filling rooms with hushed tones like suede estimates of firm direction. How the fingers want to give themselves, lean into music as it blesses atmosphere. Reaching deep into an unknown form, slide gently as an attitude.

Gravity, an energy churned slowly, homemade miracle

A Saxphone Wind Presses

Friday afternoon, islands of prayer pose insurmountable odds. Forgive each obstacle, I tell myself. A saxophone wind presses my system. I take it for granted, in the key of C. Flute mirroring prestige, a twisted treble filament coating the essence of my ring, a wedding band of mercenaries. Music winces my day's routine, inhaling singleness. I live movies I have never seen. Trumpets pressure my enclosure, taunt me. Drawerful of silk scarves. I quit smoking while too young to smoke. Now that I am old enough, I do not brush such paper to my lips. Sit on the piano, let it teach a few tunes. Play them back. Reciprocal intensity. Call in the tuner.

Instrument of life force, mouth-to-mouth resuscitation it inspires

Biography

I wanted to have equals as friends. Who knew what it was not to be undervalued, oversized, and brain dead. An assembly line of talent without pity. Eye to eye combat in the graffiti zone of inwardness transposed from space. Cryptic admission paid for by citizens favoring high functioning in public places. Bumperstickers glued to rusting metal. Driving intelligence into the outback with memory surviving like a picturebook of words and phrases deemed crystals of the language.

Litmus test of independence, lateral gravity a form of loyalty

A Tentative

Perishable heart. I've not precluded spoiling you. Is this mutual? Softness taking its cue from generations, coloratura soprano's old integrity yearning to feast its matinee tastes dutifully, a fandango. Buffalo gals, won't you let me have my say? Pragmatic incidents loom in an atmosphere of bygones zigzagging like waylaid apartment seekers hoping to furnish nests with appetizing statements, candied yams, and penitence.

Hot springs, all the not narrow bold hoops widening like topography, your health

Visualization

I memorized some words like renting less than what I would have said more beautifully. A shrine to non-experience, my loneliness cheats on itself, splits into being, an amoeba. How I enjoy the silk of conversation, white sand mirroring the gusty trees budding apart, receptacles for gentleness. The chart of one tense must reflect another brightly. I resolve the issues humanly within myself, talk to a face whose phonevoice cradles mine to sleep, as though I were a child. Wanting to gather your emotions, take them home with me in you and be at home completely. My skin containing thoughts of you not yet resolved in touch. Tattoos unprintable with passion.

Gemcrust, visual, light frost beneath the sun

Cheesecloth: Spiritual

Studio white ephemeral incubator shapeless mass geometry. How does your garden grow. Motel hot bath vacation multiplied like publisher's advance in my mind weakly panning gold in light, the cherished moments dehumidified in a basement room where spores collect unwanted. I write like a sieve accepting rinse travelling through lightspeed. Retain only the moisture then the thought of flow. Dependence upon sturdy fabric, tennis racquet microfied into proper perspective, fine eraser crumbs. Whatever happens cannot be dismissed. Archangels live inside us. We estimate our worth highly as infancy corrodes magic and a seed of permanence is planted.

Floodlights, center stage, inception of a thought

Sacrifice

The backboard animosity freed me from an obligation to pay back largo dividends like child support for fractured memories. A boomerang fed mirror told me things I never knew. Myself positioned as a prisoner accepting cuffs minus the core jewelry to ignite desire to get away. Palatially inscribed cave like the inside of my head bleating confessions from the recent past. Closed shop of hypothetical enlargements on my face. I opened up and told myself configurations that could change me.

I-thou insignia on eighteen carat love entanglements progressively unravelling

Haibun 16

As silence holds the floor, I come to agree with its calm basting of experience. Some of what it shows is like a challenge to become almost as quiet. Or to know the difference between it and myself. Myself outside of any season. Imitations left behind. So the eyes take over for a while, each a dot of ocean. Making miracles while saying nothing. Looking at each other, then looking away. Maybe for many weeks. Or months of silence, knowing the difference between echo and first word.

Aluminum sea pan, too bright for staring into, a head turns to face the sun

from

Sad Isn't the Color of the Dream

I'm Best at Playing the Game
When I'm Not Playing the Game

The little crevices
To go in
And out of

Punctuate a legacy
Of ghetto living

Seethe and slaughter
Chaperones in the value-laden
Forum of civics class
And speculum

Behold
I am not interested
In shirt tail connective
Tissue between my psyche and someone's
Creative imagery
Of the cosmos

Talk to me about original mistakes
Resplendent with humanity
A dither of fastball
Derivative conversation
Lathering post-haste minutiae
In uniform trembling

Brass aglow
With pomp encrusted
Shorelines
Granting immunity
To self-importances
Arraigned in their composite stable

A Portrait of Beverly C.

There is too much to tell in one sitting. She is not sitting she stands with her t-shirt from Harvard too large that just fits. Dipping fruited yogurt from white styrofoam on Sunday. Reading ads from Target.

Every genius needs a balance to be balanced. She is she and I observe the balance in an afternoon. Wheat in July corn in July fresh artichokes. What were we talking about.

Money for a little while. She's eating with a silver spoon from the Edna Doyle estate of which she was recipient of six silver spoons. One for ice cream and five others for the storage shed.

I ask her anything about tomorrow she says probably. And I agree having no choice except to open doors leaving a place. I place my interest extracurricularly in her face and small bones my curriculum. A xylophone of much discrete music with discretion also. The crevices between equally musical. Movies to be made and lived and made.

Sunflower

Large enough to capture light a physical wheat orange. Maybe functional or just a pool of useless in the yard. Curled petals veer from center flower padded like a sponge. Heat toughens everything about the fat weed with a face. Too large to touch. No longer pretty like a woman once. Slum jewel. Exempt that is to say from blades. Not lens or paint-brush.

Breath, emerging rainless life, collected

Some Yellows, Some Dark Blues, A Chocolate Color

Bankruptcy is full of elbow room

He decided to declare war
On boredom before depleting
His supply of energy

The radiant intrinsic value of relief
Comes as an unexpected house guest each year

Each year we learn what mountain we are climbing

Some of the shadows want to trade
Their symptoms for the sun

Each one a separate rosary bead

Each one a story of defection

Until the floor is less a safe place
Than a state of mind

Risk fluttering like wings
Tuned in to natural engagement

Some yellows, some dark blues, a chocolate color

Recall that any limitations can be danced to
In the time prescribed

Recall that pantomime detracts from love of music

Snow an afterthought, some built-in safety

Where is She Living Now

It is her boat her envelope her conversation
It is pressure not to be together then
To be together
Would she listen after all these

It is her monologue her sweatsuit her brooch
The organizational chart popping
With her centered
With her sheltering

It is her command of the terrain
Whereof she speaks the language
Having moved slowly away across years
Where she is living now

It is her wonderment
Scaling unfound places gradually
Having as her mate this gravity
Continuity to lower
This body her breath
Her statuesque
Endearment to the powers

The Question Following the Statement

Mortality camps
Out on my sidewalk
A priestly surveillance
Of preambles
To control birth
Keep it haywire and random
Celebrating pearlgate
Necklace she unwillingly
Receives

The sewer words complement
Reality I'm told
Quotidian amazements
Duck under prominent
Doorframes to get through
Faking the shit content
To be acceptable

Icicles and steam impress
Upon the forehead symptoms
Of ramified zoning
To build a home per capita
To liberate the fallow
Sandtraps from their nakedness

Line segments measure
The countdown to death
I quietly
Simmer here
Arrested by mushrooms
And new construction

Pressure

A blue
Robin egg
I think robin
Split on
Asphalt
A car going
By some
Trees olive
The moisture
Near
My thinking
What this
Has to do
With me
A distant
Sky some
Traffic
Flute all
Lidded up
Under
The pressure
Being opened
Not quite
All of it
My fault

Aspirations

I wanted to be seated at the best desk in the building to be shielded from bad news. A prime location from which mountains are so visible they look like crayon freshly smeared onto a page. I thought the view would be like reading into crystal, for the mountains are a different color every hour and I'm distracted. Quiet multiplies itself into a vast chemical imbalance where I notice everything like news delivered inside thunder. Multiple insights puncture status quo which wants to be called peacetime. Which must be taken apart to fit inside the box labeled that name.

Privacy, chapter and verse, blurred wisdom signals

A Portrait: Norm

Proceeded to talk till I was kind. About his family: daughter a physical therapist, son religious past divorce so Norm won't live with anyone. Do I, am I married. Explanation. Norm, I go on reading. Lonely till I stop, decide it's being true to instinct not the need of looseleaf to be filled in. Liberal, gentle, cooked the meals for her through 37 years. After the medical bills, worked cheap, owns merely the microwave. Her ashes. One of his relations sent plane fare. I begin to love him. Norm the next leg of my flight leaves ground without a word. I have a father.

Temper, tempered, tempering, the mangy schedule, psyche now warm enough

Sad Isn't the Color of the Dream

At night when free the skin accepts
Whatever comes the swingset does not show
It moves with grace
A lighthouse fixed apart can lift to climes
Where it would be discarded

Only the deep shell of the body loosens
As senses momentarily shut down stay
Suspended
Jackhammer steering wheel and ivy vine
Pronounce the taste of night
The smell touch hearing itself think
And poised always for magic

Use of the Generic Masculine

Her mouth and skin so beautiful
All the men especially the women want her
No better lips her skin
In confidence moves steadily
Remarks do not distract
The mouth perfectly young
Wisdom showing through her lovely eyes
When did it come
All the men especially
The women want her
How does the skin remain so soft
She is polite aloof a special animation
Silence
Mouth so beautiful
All the men especially

Overdue Books

I have come to love not having read them. The still life placed just so along my desk within the study. Darkly occupying preludes to its shadow. Many thoughts surrounding like an inspiration. Germ of entreaty blossoming near windows. Conversation piece. Gentle reminder of the possibilities forthcoming. When knowledge will appear like a desired instance of crystal. Pressure to be genuine, accepting light. The nounliness of form that genuflects to content.

Plagiarism, self-projection, one beside another

Portrait: Eleven Years

Perspiration is so beautiful a flower

❋

I watch you breathe in sleep, the oscillating fan pushes silk scarves into an atmosphere softly accepting punctuation

❋

For the first time home grows easy on the mood and spacious

❋

A reflection of magnetic red rock liberty under the influence of pure will

❋

I practice dropping tautness down into the face whose first emotion is resist

❋

Accept making the other into an image to avoid a loneliness

❋

Wallpaper taunts unformed patterns into hearing ourselves think

❋

Your leg outside the comforter just temperate enough to mix the touch for dream

❊

Each object in the house beyond appearance aura-laden, visible

❊

Jaw tries to relax, the color of our walls, an undetected strand of blue behind the white

❊

Something to picture, begin a meditation

Portrait of the Other

Adequacy teems intimidatingly
I lapse watching
Where I have not advanced
The lingering illness of non-penetration
Dagwoods upon spokes
Twisted   engaging
Like the flash of sword
In microscopic shards
Bristling under skin
Tinged entropy

My guard down
I fly in the face of every wit
Celebrate defeat
Infuse sensation
Defuse sensation
Wither

The El Dorado in the left lane
Practicum
Slashed garbage
In the trough
Dutifully pressures
To impeach duties
Impeach the status quo
Formulate Ides proliferate
Old teachers write to me
Asking remembrance

The paint I use is flawed
Gunmetal color to arrest
In paintings on the page
The father
Who bristled at discovering
I did not begin as an adult
With power to relieve me of my childhood
Bruised this face
Made spitshine of my attempting

Joy

Her facelight unconditional. Mistakes I make are jewels.
She tolerates then celebrates examination of response is see
the nature learning to be light. See fireworks attach to
sumptuous imagination. Clean waxed shining. Treefrogs in
night air transposed to peace within the body. In the body
song remaining after work infested leadership estranged from
how the human system functioning at its own helm speaking to
an interruption clearly. Pausing to take breath and become it.

Livelihood, relationship, an accidental loveliness

Meditation on Impatience

The pay channel of my productivity threatens to foreclose on
this body
Unless I lie still and render unto the world
Each vocabulary syllable entrapped
In globes of misunderstanding

What do they want of me these small firecrackers
Occupying every joint
When I move it's not a celebration of independence
My presence scuffs the paradise in which
I am an intruder
Until my brain can pacify this body
Until my blood cells can engage the flow
Not force a pinching of their space by urgency

I see a swirl like very fattening French donuts
Trying to cover flatlands of this universe
Politely as if it were possible to force a speed on God
And time creation to some criterion-referenced banana peel
On which festive heels are slipping
In the fandango symbolizing
An escape from peace

Mass at the Crypt

My father the brains of this outfit can't remember his own name or where he has misplaced the pipe tobacco, matches, eyeglasses, the pipes themselves. A man I see at football games dispenses communion by splintering the host he gives to me. As though he's changed his mind about recipience. I say "amen" astutely as though I had just learned the word. My father takes the stairs leading to moderate bright weather. Braincells each day are dying happily within him. The daughter is prepared to be both shade tree and moonlight, remedy the situation. How it works and plays.

Syllables to mean smallest prayers, the ice once broken

Falling in Love Falling in Love With You Syntax

Duties over I am
Falling in love falling in love with you syntax
Things as they might be
Once I went with sad geology
Who knew rocks not impurely
Talked of rocks touched the soul
That rocks may have
I drank a toast to new tall order
Meaning me I drank a toast
Taught him to drink a toast
Got sloshed with him
And dreamed of you prolifically
Falling in love falling in love with you syntax
Gambling away bread money
Gambling away shoe money
Gambling away approximate he-man ventures
Limited partnerships unlimited
In search of capital gain
In search of no load growth
In search of anger
Meanwhile
Falling in love falling in love with you syntax

from Teth

insinuate a thing must dream itself
woven in snow
apparently the guise of Gable
may I have this
relocation please
shovels and crew assignments
spelling bee glitch chemlab
exploit leave
to glean how much they loved you
sacrifice for verity
the nymphomaniac circumference of love
stilted unruly body television
unmarked police hum blended virtue
genuflect
the theater has precedence
over some certain sacraments
temperate enough to happen
by themselves
air in sufficient tires
to guide the road regarding
its true place

virgin prophet indigo quite deep eyes
manufactures pain
from which he'll rescue
meanwhile the relief
impresses only lean mauve veering
on white walls
comfortably enough
to be a present tense
the recent past like war
all heroes have dismantled
as rug fibers handmade
then sequestered
name your planet henceforth
rise to the occasion
violet tufts
immaculate cream skin
as pretense heralds for the comfortable soul
first home enunciated thirst
luster and chimney nestled
as the signals branch
toward an unclaimed sea

refrigerator transforms
poached pear
into fiberglass
all winter
wanted distributive
warm socks noble endurance
traditional in season
ever perjuring
anomaly from happening
the blue discursive incident
so blond it's truly happy
misspelling from hell appliances
significant difference at the .05 level
my harmonica's abrasive thumbtone
patriots are out of style
their schoolwork is infested
with numb logic don't forget
to request a transfer then
remember to get out after remembering
to pull the cord tell the driver story of line
segment

borscht akimbo during vodka
I remember freedom
looking through the wavy glass
water pressure
clean remark
professor chapped and bald
seeking the adoration
of lean mineral experience
hometown street pinch
something of real life
amend routine pleasure a comb
small frame
to exhaust perspective
chance redemption
be prepared to lose
the whole investment
guarantee
a 25% return
the golf entreaty joyride
slender tip light
until bathtub ignites the warm club
fifty anything in round numbers
manipulate sweet cauldron
temporary jaded silo

mahatma fox I call her reverentially
as gladiator forces evil their intention
in pursuit of home to me
demystify the scoundrels
sanctifying blood
they use to dye their clothes
at a tremendous cost per wearing
in contrast to her one
froth colored soul extension
a persuasive emblem of interior
reflect rejection syntax
even as it blushes so bystanders
if they do exist can view
and draw conclusive
sustenance plaited
and fully soothed somewhere
within the riddle
no one has to pose

long distance breastmilk
unrequited symptom
holy swimming pool menagerie
the pilgrim children never mine
menstrual cavity resolved
again societal detention
the one instance
I bought baby food for us
a vegetarian simplific spree
enclave of easy
for the weeks that we could stand
no sodium at all
no interest
they smiled warmly
from cash register
less to my cash
than a condition fictive
being wanted by a stranger
and redeemed for her
a mother to me anyone
allow me to self-introduce

per our agreement thistling
mo-mantra fresh Monmartre the metro tube
this river of my neck
mind wizened coal shock of the cheekbone
shave and shore alike
say blink
the man semester hides
in blue book
it is the dismal
Thursday kind of blue
kings wish were drought occasionally
consistently the tucked in frame
alongside risk
newborn repeat signs
surname hemline blood
pose cleared for prescient creekbed
pathing trance into a keepsake
trembles cave of small print
telepathic art museum
fully vested

tome is wisecrack sketched alive
say intuition bore resemblance
to an audience
created of its wisdom
purge straightjacketed proforma
dizzy with untimely lack of rescue
muscleshirting its way
into the voting crowd
of bright light habitat
to register plumb saturated
with maternity
as a for instance
to dismember stations of the cross
memory bank plenty symmetrical
with shabby out-takes
glass persona ritually personal
all saved ahead as green stamps
could be licked into a book
exchanged for a Corvette or something

is she radiant
oh plenty plenty
she remakes me
at my sincere request
I sometimes glean
when frame shops form the portrait
make an offer
push collective fork
into the food
collective wine
I serve them palpable
with more future results
the mysteries all solve themselves
and partake channel osmotic center spree
let me then sleep beside her temperature
symphony also capable
of infinite performance
this room is pet once
though I digress beyond peyote
open the radio and speak back

learn the womb can't love
enough
select a new
ill-fitting section of the planet
to reside in
claim your heart
frost legged ready to be tried
searing the disappointment
of failed bakery
consistently on empty
holy thistle
on the law
most sanctified
longhand bouquet
mesmeric charity
with glitter still residing
in the comb
whose bristles score some touchdown
like variable plantation mummies
held responsible for apprenticed crops
depressive until certain hunger
she ventriloquist amazingly
appoints herself guru
of failed light
supposing

gendarmes inside remember
proper place
shell crypt pose dangerous
bloodstream
torn to years voiced adios arrangements
norm and silo
classic feather of a man
preponderance
grilled lambent
alloy hock
and poll pop fictive strum
the baste is twitching
in the zero yard unruly pep
diseased and atrophied
part cocker and part rain
slyly composed of imperfection
sealant or developments inimitable
next door features avenue
plantain whose hunger
loose changed daylights
into something mental like a porchlight
in the sentence he illumined

maybe we project our little village
onto philanthropic squares
of canvas obbligato
temple mention
zoom lens
racial prejudice
award winning concupiscence
I wake tomorrow
my dilemmas solidly intact
tight fitting reasonable assurances
that there will be a day
the mystics cry for untapped
amazing hemisphere
raw face
unleavened muscular control
blurred scope of inference
crazy germane boy resonance
his helper
cryptic cipher jellybean
mind you devalued currency
at last entrepreneurial
resisting the temptation
to cease being prideful
small
informed of consequence

preambular morning
if I speak to melody around me
dump truck
slaphappy birds
exhaust
some weakly snarling pets
uncoffeed humans
sponge headphones
pleat the sense of hearing
grapefruit imperceptibly fall juicy over lawns
divestiture the headlock
ounces me in sensibility
live antenna branches
fortify lawn minerals at night ahead
core epoch seethes pronouncement
morning glory sifts edges
of imposter ruins
voice chain link protection
from the mass without possession
of enough imagination to transcend
sound
corrupted how the mind is
music

yacht floats on 80 proof
those breezes
one woman's heaven
is another's vain equestrian confusion
hamper stovepipe love
riding the spelling of the syllable
a word for beautiful
in French masculine
shelter we connipted over rent check
every bristled angel uncorked
bottles of her rage
tipped and poured into white empty face
empty with death
whose plastic surgery refined
an image of perplexity
the fossils very winded
have incorporated planning
into every feeble motion
left within the will
the color *jaune*

casual with words
lace picnic
features open curtain
bristled sage pacemaker
alcohol in sufficient quantities
begins to temper love
your family has for you
allotted mainstream bone structure habitat
the normal curve
bathing elaborately night
a fact day lily
stubble ruckus who's the bird
appears to preach headlong white sentences
into a cup
the ownership of instruments
become a sex to call your own
and hound the talk show hosts
with plenty virtue and descriptors
sanctimonious until they fit
complicit strictures

logic mostly snatches birds
from every audience
they stipple envy
the pronunciation of tattoo
street clogged with whores
now clean and blank
a has-been office
cylinder appeasement
like the farm
say something
like tape measure
itself
bake white ham
call rabbit carry wish
the foot
and term it luck
buy tickets for the lottery
win mild sachet
to put in nylon drawer
wear proudly even though
the company that sells them insists
on misreading "Dr."
and always
addresses your invoice "Sister"

hysterical post-rain mockingbirds
sound lost toward midnight
I sit between silk indoor plant
and an expensive lamp
so warm that I pronounce arthritis dead
the walls contain no spawned art
but what I calibrate on site
from the folding chair to mimic
masters yet unborn
who will dissolve
the canon for a version
plenty sentiment warm carpet
dry moonlight stops being Romantic
Cuba is a song
is to be sprinting over
touched up blacktop dallying
with open air a sought possession

virtually pinned to incapacity
he notices without distraction
guestbed brittle sexuality
gnawing hunger for hard tack
itchy woodsy planetary get lost
where the javelina roam
blind to our fear of them
and lunging circumspectly
because out of balance
see how nourishing
even wind can be
an off night
the cicadas
proving ownership of spaces
to which we apply
the metal tape measure of obligation
sorting what is recommended
from plantation obbligato
twiddling musical enough thumbs
false fronting luminous calamity
alias nature

accept then weave the center
into body nerves emotional
weave graphic litmus
mention this foremost snapshot
rendered masterpiece
whose pure contralto melts all
sex and urgent armor
dying for significance
whose rope and chime
define the fanfare of a neighborhood
whose swingsets cheapen kinaesthetic jamboree
squeaks liven the yard and sacrifice
of purity as canon echoes
what the elders thought worth saving
in mindrealm charitably rendered
mindloom fastens new craft
to pathways previously unsigned
and kept sequestered
broadjump talent
permanent rehearsal

ideogram
notes of the scale
coat hanger
do you take this pinesmell
fairly dilapidated trailer
I mean motor home
to be your permanence
the wisp of cell condition
breathing through the nose and mouth
the gateway slow paced
leftist correspondence
course waitlisted
heap of grandeur
lingering design curve
mention handmade woodwind instrument in France
you'll have an argument
concerning reeds and bailing wire
red to contend with
what do you make of
one mascara colored sock
left in the middle street

indebtedness tips guilt
swish nearly to the full abrasive
right face
where sir
I am yes sir
taking your orders sir
all the while aware of grief
the color
grief the touch
and grief the template
sacrosanct enough to breach
a blender salvo
do you take this core apostrophe
to be your signal of intrusion
certain acquiescence
winking tissue farms out aim
and misses crucial lines
that once were segments
then extended their opaque domain
grew clear enough to follow
blended

trousers and holster with tools
very functional
this home healed
and intimidate
point of unnatural
casting a pot redemption
the elements hardened
to form them into objects
worth possessing
our home
is a crop
and my body
sleeps late here's the movie
I'm living in silence
apology flute speech
coarse animal hair
of the bow on this fiddle
serene as all coupons do flow
so disarmingly
value unburdens itself
of the dailies
and charm redistributes
its potting soil
over scarred surface

inspires regret
the muscle of lead pipe
simultaneously read about a purity
in India namely
bathe the enemy in unconditional love
bowl resonant with light
the color of a chapter
I would treat gestures
uncommonly complex to untangle
warty little hedonist
who shimmied up the corporate greased pole
on someone else's wits
about to fall
teach self no response
the empty swimming pool
a fact of spectacle
the dry dry afternoons without relief
relentless air conditioning
exceeds even
the muscle expectations

digital clockface summons me
on signal "10:05"
childhood address
I may be thinking then
some cure for maternal grief
it comes waving suggestive energy
in my wide open face
consider the masseuse
whose full bruised body
sacraments her craft
as innocence enduring actively this world
athletic fingers
nothing accidental about cold
pressed oil
slathered across
tight muscles of the lower back
that yield tuned answers
to unasked questions this cool canvas
is to be your world
what will you name it

from

Tommy and Neil

from first section: Tommy

This collection of poems was written in honor of my brother Tommy's 36th birthday. Each of the 36 poems was written in three passages, consisting of 54, 13, and 6 words, respectively, to celebrate the date of his birth: June 13, 1954.

- SEM

Playpen caged your beauty.
All I knew was movement without dance.
I tossed in toys that clogged the space
Until you could not move.
I talked with no one to talk to.
Talked to flowers and the raspberries.
Talked to cherry trees while climbing.
Sun gleamed in your red curls in the back yard.

Yellow flowers shaded just enough not to grow crisp do not slightly move.

I postpone our lifelong tender conversation.

Touched his head.
Uncle said don't touch.
I said he is my brother.
Loved his newborn beauty, head, closed eyes.
How small a statue with such moves.
How very hands love them, their skin.
His eyes, the brother entering a name.
The retrospective soul, a man.
Such patches of the waking life that shields.

Ordered a brother, soft curls red, and face a glowing newborn angel, warm.

To see boy settled man now.

Cherry trees were tall.
A memory enlarges small things
Toward disappointment, later years.
A white colored fence
Beyond escape,
The orchestration difficult.
The world a grab bag
Of mismatched dance steps.
If we dance it is in broken pieces.
Certain light shimmers
On rocks beside the harbor.
First knew emptiness,
Your poised sad face.

To seem whole, I asked for you when there was nothing.
Tulips bloomed.

From letter distance I am made.

What does water soothe?
How does the lapping tone affect the skin?
How is the skin protective?
In the night water surrounds, accepts surrounding
As the sphere not entered.
Ask temptation round.
My brother is a calm though warm momentum.
Often he is close-the-eyes,
The eyes close,
Water lapping every sentence long.

Does the water soothe, supposing an eraser of a form of water lapping?

Does the water soothe, the water?

Mother's potato salad made with pickle juice and mustard
In a bowl atop the illustrated picnic tablecloth
With freedom in the shape of firecrackers
Printed over it.
The mind performs roll call on rustic looking strangers
Claiming to be friends
Until it's dark enough
To watch light be distributed
In streams that quickly die.

Existential melodies smell like percussion in a rainbow topping all the charts amenably.

Popularity, a form of birth order

You watched him bark decades of hatred,
And my armor stiffen
As his hand exploded in my face,
The same instant that love connected with protection
Died.
Spokes of the escape wheels spattered steely rays
Along the street, patches of helpless longing.
We grow up shaped unfair, our families
Enormous in their latent referentiality.

What did the short repeated scene look like from all the way outside?

You wear his interrupted younger face.

Tosca might have been the opening
Releasing a lament with grace,
The little look you get when someone disappoints
Your tenderness, impinges on the distance
Between you and potential comfort
For security makes every sense emotionally.
You have always seen the hidden beauty
In a growing thing, even when withering became the norm.

An aria requests the supple bandages that may invite
themselves to surface calm.

The intellect chiefly hurtful, although tender

Tears want to be your tears, then my tears.
They are promiscuous with kindness,
Shape our world the color wand
To which each one of us has access.
I tell the story: you relive.
You tell the story: I relive.
They fuse into root happiness
As everyone who breathes would fear
A sentence opening.

The sight of you in frame wearing a wounded look infused with clarity

Your singing voice, pure wooden flute

My conscience takes you in the arms of what I've made of life
And plants pure pleasure, trust, good things.
Our minds safe in a room that is the world.
The world a perfect garden,
Not restrictive playpen bars,
But dance.
Imagine dance so quietly,
A likely pure event,
True to the imagined life.

Articulate disruption in the mind between her face, the face of lonely planet

And similarly quiet room, loved one

You reflexively seem able to forgive.
I still hold guilt
As though a ransom note that stings the hand.
Nettles of discipline offer
Freedom from pain. Focus yields
Needed compliance.
If we were to turn back
And I poured generosity like constant baptism
Across your forehead, would you learn to still be new?

Play consistently seems work. Work often is easy.
Movement wears unbuttoned, open texture.

Will to be myself with me.

Bluish wood along Australian highway
Where gum trees and pine
Erupt patches of dark fractions.
Sense of this world glows
Like the most endearing evidence
That a collective renders under beauty
All selfhood, mild possession melody.
A caper is the circumstance of love,
A kind possession,
Booze inside the fire we watch glow.

Breath energy to mention broken moments, the paralysis of sentences turned mantra, cope

In the restaurant mutual pain consumes

Having preceded your world
Past an amenity
(Sequence means nothing),
Little loved one of the eyes who shields me,
Glad to see you cared for,
Glad to see a happy shell around old innocence
Protectively immersed in any image
That suggests your happiness.
The emptiness extends its hand to you.
I am that emptiness.

Among flowers, the June yard, born to warmth, so even love was calm.

Eroticism, the conviction we are wanted

I write from a proximity, the long sleep in your home.
A guest here, I am family.
The past supplanted by this
Namesake of reality.
The now where we are always friends
Entwined in love,
Extend within your eyes
Full antecedent to the words:
Happy (a frequent mention of it)
Birthday (yours) my life.

Tiny message in my skin already secret, touch equally
ephemeral is reason feeling.

And in a thoroughbred sound sleep

Choice I'm always not touching,
Though monuments silhouette instead the life,
A giant partnership attention game
All particled
With labels and zippers and spray paint.
There aren't any vestiges.
This time around I'd know exactly what to do with Escanaba:
Write you letters to reclaim my sanity.
Sleep late into the sentence,
Live, explain.

A seam in the form of dental floss invisibly connects us over water.

Hand-drawn figure, blue ink, red curls

from

Tommy and Neil

from second section: Letters to Neil

I *wrote Letters to Neil shortly after my brother Neil had relocated to Phoenix, where I had then lived for 16 years. The book, a gift to him on this 36 years, consisted of 36 individual letters.*

Before you could speak, Dad called you his *consultant*. Declared the need to hear your views. Would whisper something in your ear, purport to decode garbled unformed syllables, then tell Tom and me, "My consultant thinks it would be dangerous and that I should not let you go." We fell for that a few rounds and got mad at you instead of Dad.

The youngest has to hurry and be old. You were the one to bring grandchildren home. Remain in Indiana. Watch the proceedings try to hatch. Be attentive to dysfunction without breaking.

I learn that people feel intensely more than they reveal. Your humor breezes by, distracts from pain. We teach ourselves to pantomime a way to feel without completely healing. Sun evaporates from drear leaves in the autumn when nostalgia stretches to achieve loving remembrance.

Thematic whine of *Little Rascals*, you in foreground light consuming Cream o' Wheat. Porch curtains open all around. Raw miniature voices offer each of us an easy home in friendship. Buckwheat's peaceful smile, Alfalfa's eagerness, the cowlick. Spanky with the dog. All primed to register the love of *hearing it again* and seeing in routine what is emotional string music. We weave a neighborhood around this comfort, interrupt no breath within our world. No belly laughs, just mild surprise laced with the violins. The seasons frame each nest of personality established and uncluttered in soft places where a life is formed.

We worry as a pair. Reflect on what might go awry, already has. I can be sure of liking music that you like. Modes consonant with skin draw out an impulse to absorb Metheny or the sound track to those Snoopy specials I should know the name of. We listen with the same skin. Hear homonyms as chords combine with some loose line of melody. And symmetry forms legislation of connective grief with the economy of string and ritual. Tundra in our hearts, the lasting change of warming. A melody scripted for toss into another way of sensing. Celebration of new growth and tactics.

You invited Jimmy Carter to our house to celebrate your college graduation among neighbors and mock orange levity. Layers of social class and age were like a crafted torte. The light of relatives' emotion. Years of friendship open to the tempting future. Carter didn't come. Security, the reason. Schedule. But a letter came, official, that you framed.

When you were six, you took your school photograph to Mr. Henningfield, the Principal, told him you knew he'd want one. Mr. Henningfield retold the story many times. So did our parents. All your life, a celebration of the selves around you.

After Dad had been at Notre Dame some thirty years, people approached to ask if he were Neil Murphy's father. Dad retold that one, too. An engine proud of its caboose. Reversal in so many ways. Father and son.

Members of the John Adams High School band played in the stands like a collective sitting duck. What surface craft its marches owned before the strife came. It was a toasty summer, fall. Boys who carried leather cases with band instruments were bloodied en route home. You decided that a mouthpiece was not worth it with life tentative. The races hardly spoke to one another. Any contact appeared impudent. What boundaries there were eroded. For a while, your friends rehearsed the role of enemy. Swollen feelings lingered while we heard there were no answers.

You would dance inside the flashlight prattle. Strobe to fine-tuned glisten of direct address. Spark-laden dance sequenced to wrist flick. White legs swan-cool ashimmer in mild darkness. A falsetto quivering. Each speck of applause, a fitful prelude to as much serenity as youth could glean. Legs, fingers, face inside imagined movie all across centrific lifeline.

People use your name as avocation. Hub of spokes that make a neighborhood. Each new thing you think with kindness. Coin dispensers made of cardboard just a whit off center. Spliced wires to accommodate more phone extensions than are legal. You invent what isn't glamorous and people come to it like hot springs. Leaves spatter in a cycle, yogic unto selves that like you. Listen to what's possible, a centered happiness. Blue eyes, long lashes. Beard that mentions present tense is not long for this world.

Dad would discuss stocks, options, and the mutuals with Tommy and then ask you, "How's Shuman?" Considered you a burst of fireworks with lovely heart. Recently, your self-driven portfolio swelled 41%. Instinct runs on praise. You think what income will be like three months from now. What stocks will be a found poem in fine print. Impossible to second guess you. A voracious interest in short cuts and playthings. Choices about to fall from trees proclaim ripeness like absolution.

You empty the hot pipe against Dad's music box ashtray. As he would do while still able to light a match. The divestiture of clarity happens slowly. As curtains of this house surrender to unwinding tune. The smell of oak leaves burning in an autumn wind. I replay conversations with a ghost who must comprise a prayer. The sort of offering that makes peace with weapons before being calmed. Addressing what it means to climb up out of middle distance.

Twelve years ago in March the weather for your marriage sparkled an unseasonable flash of light. The photograph possesses a soprano look equated with the pale peach colored dresses. Ben was a tiny child and bore the ring. You were smooth looking, handsome. Cameras flashed. Our relatives partook of food, and it was time to postpone dying. All nervousness and smiling. Our hope mutual for no shame. A day like petals of the flowers seeping oxygen, esteem.

I like you and your handshake. Love you and the baseline in your deep connective tissue voice. The land appreciative around you. Children gone to their secure sleep loving who you are to each round laughter. Each springsong. Sonata. How wisdom is accrued and will remain handsome like conscience. People love your swimming pool blue eyes. Are drawn to gentleness and kissest light. You offer and proceed to sing. These burning signals to the headset sun.

Was I an event you watched that would not speak? A head start of four years sequestered me. You were not real until I slowed into the hammock of adulthood. My flute, a complement to piano keys of yours and saxophone. I sensed an urgency about maturing. A race toward acquisition of a value system almost no one could afford. You represented pleasure in a size too young, too small. I equated peace with safety from surprise. Enjoyed days over easy. Potential homebody watching you nudge wires to find voices plain spoken. And concoct home versions of machines that charmed you. We waited years to talk, beginning in the basement on the brown couch where the ironing once was. You offered proof of an awareness that convinced me of protection for the heart. Mutual and lasting, consequential.

You prepare somebody lateral for a promotion and feel disappointed by the lack of gratitude s/he can't afford. The poor in spirit have no slush fund of ability or magic. What little they possess is bloated to prove out regression to the mean. Meanwhile, true ability squirms under the mute button. You spend what chits you have on forwarding someone's career in liberation. So success must be defined as being left alone, and seeming to accept the fact of hurt and waste. All creased and starched in linen white.

How do you work, and do they love you there? Your voicemail calls the receptionist by name for times you can't be reached. No inflection pleads dull or insensitive. Life goes rollicking along between lightness and long attention span that places customers beside your heart. Soothed by contagious comfort and pronouncing virtues that we see amid conditions that refuse to hold still.

You stood on Central Avenue before the skyscraper you occupy by day, your red beard clipped and shining in the last rays of the sun. I liked again the atmosphere around you, nerve impulses feeling for the light. You waved me into the garage. I felt my humor everywhere. We toured your office. I breathed in your mood. The wooden Notre Dame bookends I had not seen since childhood were on your desk. It was late March. I could think nothing but the pleasure of your light around me woven like soft yarn, the sweet parade of mutual recall.

from

Pure Mental Breath

Blossom, synonymous with curfew for a change,
Whose waxen petals portend impending emptiness.
Cryptic beatitude that lingers like a chant in memory.
What are the chances that the color coral will maintain
A lifelong freshness recommended as a flower?
To personify a plant is sacrilege according to my father,
Who adores mostly the roses in my mother's garden.
What sense does it make to refrain from praying
For repose of the soul of a dead animal beside the road?
Blossom synonymous with central beauty
Of the color coral in a rose. A lifelong freshness
Of its soul. What sense did it make to stifle
Prayer? My father was not comfortable,
I think, with flower portraits of O'Keeffe.
Voluptuous
As tissues of a woman's soul: her skin
Ablossom with the rest she had
Last night when mooncoins dripped into her hand.

Balcony, the sea, a wave of siren.
Dogs howling by the sea
To equalize the tones, match indigo
This distance from the spread of sea.
A leisurely endorsement of salt air,
Of taste, your touch, this lovely morning.
Wash of tresses seafoam siren plaits
The strands of air, a silo feeling.
All sufficient memory supplies
The rampant skydive distance
From real living haze at perfect early hour.
Taste: peach, key lime. Taste cleansing
Grief in lungs, the healthy chemistry
Again, a reason to display
Such feeling history
From lifelong easy balcony
Earned, the guilty coating
Over energy, then plush seafoam, wave of siren.

Parentheses keep us warm.
Maybe one of them, a new fence, opens
Other avenues. Maybe turned the other way
Parentheses would seem obstacle to a pruned,
Deliberate seeing What flows in the stream of thought
Accepts an ordered closure
Suggestive party favor
Endured to earn socialization
To satisfy the need for acreage
In the sparsely furnished soul,
Whose latticework accepts.
A musical review of silence newly glistens
Like a gallery on first seeing.
The tenants in their speckled frames
Terribly jolly, forthright even,
In the eyes of some new majesty
With teeth sawed off enough to frighten
Warbling pigeons signalling each other underneath the eaves.

Road becomes so instantly metonymy,
It sings when tires grind over it
With new firm grips that hug each chunk
Of cinder, gravel stone.
Road mentions politely that you need not stay
Inside your lovely or depressing home.
For to remain in motion is its own libation.
Being free, its own libation. On the road
Semesters feed into the novel you are making
Of the movement. Cities flicker by
Like little dots of charity, they feel so
Numb and harmless from this distance.
Only the whine of motor against pavement
Furnishes a lovely humming noise
We say is roadnoise meaning it sings
Under our touch as we would want
The town to do, the house,
Even if holding still possessed the same intrigue and magic.

Compose a white chenille bedspread.
Compose a hasty though appropriate address
To greet the new ambassador.
Compose wheat and lace it into finch breath.
Compose wood for hobbies meaning balsa
Catches underwind so perfectly,
The glide is easy on enduring shadow.
Part of this world awaits cleansed
Miracles to feast on,
As collateral chastens a sweet deal,
Even after signing.
Compose lifelong flute music for the prince
Whose mind flutters with
Energetic toeprints
On the walk. Compose fragments
Of necessity, aesthetic
Mines of luxury to be unearthed and finally
Exposed to perfect composition.

Tender knows the power of its hand
Requires restraint like justice. Pulls back
Against the grain
Of wanting to intrude because of need
Or excess energy. The quiet promise
Being so much even feeling
Rotates give and take again.
Until the layers tuned to intimate exchange
Run deep enough to reach the soul.
The purest center that must never be approached
Without a quiet reverence. Lines
Drawn without the hand
Of understanding. Or they never are
Acknowledged. The less attention paid
To boundaries, the more natural justice
In a combination of attracted souls
On the brink of letting go of artificial markings
To allow true melody its voice.

Amiable mention seabreeze.
Amiable companion.
How do diary pages go from memory
To the next?
Amiable keyboard pling F7 chord
Inclusive of surprise.
Then registers a note to fill in
What one wondered.
Framed excuse for emptying the distance
Of all foreground,
Carefully regretting undesired invasion,
The perfect gentleman response to woman.
Sacred me with gloves and pensive car.
She feather boa,
Or khakis hiding behind desert muted green.
Amiable the telling and from memory,
Close to sky empathic though not
Part of sky.

Strawberry tenders resignation of the universe
Unless someone visionary listens
And dispels that outcome from the chain of probabilities.
The least likely effect of sunshine is unhappiness.
Strawberry accumulates our latent energies,
Pronounces advocate long "a,"
A verb to celebrate.
That means strawberries are ripe now
For the 38th time.
The seeds within its skin endure the bite
Releasing juice
Preserved until the proper privileged teeth
Can open individual ripe being,
Sacrificed as lamb so aimless by the riverbed.
Now with purpose given from outside
An aspect of imbued freshness imparted
By the atmosphere completely taken
With an energy supposing ripeness from a perfect red.

Croquet is being symptomatic in the yard
Of bourgeois dreams. I'm telling you the range
Of human intervention within nature stiffens
Like a sapling past its definition.
Maybe clouds can be heard wishful in the case
Of pure imagination overload, the way we farm out
Particles of wish to make them true
In neighbors' minds. I see white trousers
Chalking up the lush green lawn
Pocked with occasional percussion of a mallet
Knocking smooth balls
Through a wire hoop. The afternoon completely
Civilized, testosterone on hold so paradisaical
That mention would disturb perfection
It seems in the mind, luxuriously easy
For the few fed charming soft or crisp hors d'oeuvres
Selected to maintain
Consumer's perfect weight, low level stress.

Substance missing from charisma. What's the fuel
To be sustained from a mysterious *within*?
Perhaps a memory of reasons for performing
Anything beyond choke cherry violet or forsythia
In the post-winter yard.
A core that blends physical particles
With pure mental breath.
Connection to the source, the failure to be ensconced
In football games.
Or draw distinctions between worth
And entertainment skillfully as is required
For being living in their world,
As the most leisurely bard would have it.
Substance not to measure but to draw from,
As resuscitation in emergencies
Seems a package deal, includes salvation
You had never planned on,
But accept as it is given.

Rain isn't what I like, it's no relief to me
To have sun slip behind a patch of cloud
And soften what was vibrant atmosphere
Into something I can look through
And not feel the sting, or seem
A new roof to hide under.
Rain supposed to be a miracle feels too available.
I touch its face awhile without romance.
I let rain bead on me, consider plush towels.
Rain and I don't get along
The way sun masters me.
I like baking skin intact.
I like dry atmosphere for easy breathing.
I don't like rain.
I thrive on light. In Arizona
Where a hundred days of brightness run
Like a show captures awards
Without the ritual embarrassment of public cleansing.

Surprise is chariot of the unconscious
Engineering brain with roses to replace the tumult
And a toy train advertises
The correct perspective. Daylight handed out
In spoonfuls to the deserving.
Until there is conviction that love feels
Motivation to be love without a prompt.
Someone awake for you prepares
A morning meal. It's easy to lie down and trust
You're not the only brain alive.
Each other soul is in possession of a hemline
Slowly being raised or lowered.
Intimacy breaks the chain of loneliness
In the midst of shattering
Predictable old-fashioned timing.
This comes after this comes after this.
Until the pilgrimage feels wasted
And you long to start your own.

Breath moves sacred through my being.
Trickles of bird breath, water heating on the stove,
Reduced backpain, my breath
Solution to unhappiness sufficient quiet breath.
As happiness breath music, as amazement.
I thought healing was external light.
Breath rather is healing God life.
Breath's own sacredness, even potassium,
Magnesium, fresh vegetables, oxygen.
The deeper oxygen in sacred breath.
Song of my breathing, several measures rest,
An airplane overhead movement of branches.
Blossoms, consciousness within my arms
Against the kitchen table, breath
Awareness light, the answers to uneasy
Questions. Breath the timezone, breath
Superior, interior, anterior. The full spectrum
Of past, present, in the future, breath.

Legend pores over itself dissecting the timetable
Of inception. Hoop skirt ringlets, sawed-off shotgun,
The slow drag of a wagon brittle-wheeled easing along
Unceasing absent highway. Formed by compass
Whose life force sparks from certain definition
Sans humility. The dry terrain, the nothing-happened
Line of thought about the trip.
Sparse conversion mostly emphasizing
Names for things and hardy verbs
Composed of purposeful low grunts
Bereft of any artistry, the way a pigeon
Differs from the shimmering wide pheasant
In the heresy of speech-as-comfort.
Little water, little tenderness and even
Little solitude, strangely, for always
The stern wire of connection to the lives
That duty robs of interest
In the name of mere existence.

Percussion *is* without anointing itself true
Unless hormonally imbalanced persons have it.
Then the pocketful of seeds is asked forcefully
To become watermelon, despite whatever visions
Thought prudent,
Perception may include a flash
Rendered with speed and lightness
Of a feather duster. Strokes
That cleanse the surface without punishment.
Each inkling leads away to where it is
Nurtured. As footprints held fast in cement
To aid memory in distinguishing
Among the pages of a calendar of cartoons.
Programming acceptance
Of the things to follow
Starting with seeds
That take their natural course,
Despite our nudging toward accumulated health.

Clarity mimes truth surreptitiously
Until unleavened answers pressure syntax
To be more empathetic, less simple perhaps,
As beautiful winged insect motion trembles
Atmosphere. Straight line depreciation
Connotes downhill embarrassment
For what we have become, Midwestern accent
Set on Eastern Standard Time, preferring all the while
Mountainous West, the short haul of red rock
To immortal soul. Beauty equals flow.
A license to be truthful,
Full baritone laugh ashamed of nothing.
Sequestered evidence
Of moonlight shafts some livelier appellate court
Where vibes are played one-handed
On the treble ivory
Nearing extinction fate assumes
So gracefully as things begin happen.

Neighborhood extends the reach of harmony perplexing
To outsiders who measure
The effect of mountains or proximity of houses.
Or the years spent in formation,
Planting step before next step.
Although relationship combines
Components that extend themselves mysteriously
To equal how it feels to live here.
Response to the woman who resides
Upstairs, her conception of the transients
Who leave through a collective will.
Screen fully open to improvement,
A responsibility we own together
In our separateness, the anger over dogs
Intruding on well kept front lawns,
The lazy masters absent
On the day conscience was taught.
A common enemy stokes mutual need.

Self economizes on a definition.
Declares *the flute* an adequate response
To catechism question: Who are you?
Patterned after *Who is God?*
(Reply) *God is the supreme being who made all things.*
Why would I single out a rote response
As suitable for framing, when the temperature
Of heartbeat daily changes? And routine,
Delicious as it sometimes seems,
Bows down before exceptions, hoping into life
A formula for mispronouncing
Self and purpose, path.
There is a variable ingredient about
Discovery. Newly invented soul
Changes with light each hour
Along our mountain. Averts
A fixity that understanding would impose.
Opens the room of light to self inspection.

from

A Clove of Gender

from Section I.

The Weight and Feel of Harps

The Weight and Feel of Harps

Your arms (the swish glissando lovemake. Wordless. Spinet turned along its side. The notes, mainstay amid most untrapped...scars unlace themselves from scars. Last night Venus, Jupiter, the onomatopoeia moon. A nonexistent need (only the mind to feel. A brush of arms unclothed. Vowel sounds occur to skin. Near effort might be soul. Wings momentarily reclining.

Roasted something, roses crisp, the glisten, morning roses

Would be a Father Noiselessly

Would place the cottage cheese with peach half on the top most neatly on the plate so it would be a sweet adventure to approach that evening. He would clean as he went countertop the meal would never be exciting but approachable. Would say things fun to hear and fun to say. The way words went. Would imitate Richard C who sounded prissy and precise. Would point forefingers toward the sky and kick one foot behind him in a festive dance. Would spring a little gesture to his walk. Would smile sweet imitative face. Would seem happiness would be a father noiselessly. Clean pans one at a time while Mother and I walked. Would interrupt no program with thought process. Read *The South Bend Tribune* with a fleck of interest. Read some mystery and like its being solved. Like better sounds of words the way they happen to enjoy the things they signify. All the moments he would remake to learn enjoyment. Moments he'd forget. Sound of the flute his daughter's flute. Sound of the open holes ringing with practice. Open windows facing Howard Street the summer afternoons. The lilt they gave to practice.

Shepherd the estrangement, altitude, beach sand between the toes, the ready-made appearances

The Lullaby of Sun

That I be the plant she feeds sunlight (palmilla) with sufficient water stored, with light. Sufficient play given to wingstones. Laughter. Sill to cover. That I be the plant she seeds again.

And hikers form a flow of scenery trespassing. Water shakes and spills percussion that reminds me they are coming. Drops of water I can store.

Sufficient water to be played the lullaby of sun, the lullaby caress-with-eyes. The lullaby a mother. I am fast asleep, cared for by low voice singing, safe within her arms.

Plenty of sun to look the way I am. This distance from a path. And bees, onlookers. Arms encircle me. Their warmth, my warmth also.

Beautiful Sunwarm Arizona
Beautiful Absence of Crimes Against the Skin
Beautiful Sleep to Open Sky Motif
Beautiful Lovemake to the Hum of Sky

Moreover I'm suspended in this moment of your tenderness
I would prefer to keep
Would rather glean from certain moccasins
The shape and feel of elements
We wide awaken
As the soft mid-air detains an underpinning
Shaped like sadness
Any accident is pleasure
To the tune of frame the tune of holy ropes we know
We sleep

Moreover I'm agreed to love in theory and
The practice is my fondest symptom
Mercury slips out of retrograde at last
At last the homonyms
Are starting to be neighbors and the tulips speak
Hibiscus will prevail they match my mother's hair
The season is a relic of efficiency and spree
The bliss of it inside
The net accommodation furnishing the seaside moon
Until my mood is glandular again

Moreover I'm sensate as youth despite
The several whitesprouts showing I can make elastic
Of convictions now and love cement
While seeing water curdle in the stumps of seafoam
Slithering along the rhythm toward and back
So tactful as to be this version reverence

Immaculately world as we define the envelope
We need around our shoulders picture
Heaps of white warming the shamefaced chill
A full semester until sundown when another beauty
Is quite suddenly again affordable

from

A Clove of Gender

from Section II.

Informal Logic

A Pint of Training Wheels

The infant in a moo moo chevrons bursal sacks of moods. Each coffer learns to sing rambling in love to love. This place we hitch a ride. This Christ. This warm excuse for an exclusion. Walls metaprotectionist deride their actuality. A monsoon beckons, hurts. Table of foes with friendly reputations. Easter comes to life all by itself. The niche market we are, crumb weary though accustomed. Who performs the teaching task associated with survival. Thinking does not constitute real work.

Informal Logic

The box is what they said of where the toe goes. I have always thought of that as shoe, as mirror of the body part it houses. Say considerable girth and smokestack and alumnae were in dresses bloomed. Softness of bed became at once political. My grasp of the core issues, lethal. Everywhere to turn slipped into moods comprised of elements. The game of bocceball. Or thunder, some preventive aspect that nukes inclinations to be swollen, strong. Resilient word for inland policies. Sentenced to plasticine derangements. You would think or you would fail to think. The taste of cereal felt pale brown. Gossip with all its faults formed substitute clauses for the hemline of a park. Bladed along with stickers on unfeeble parts. Birch looking even with the major text erased. I like the thought of freedom better than the early taste of it. Seduction is so pretty and uncommon. He wrote a postcard and I thought of her. It was the flowers ripe upon shellacked appearing front. Each time he thinks of me a flute song ripens. All of our awake hours have to glisten what they like. They like the sound of us. And taste what isn't anything of light. Why don't we frame it and go home that is to say construct a home beside it.

from

A Clove of Gender

from Section III.

Desert Wildflowers

Desert Hibiscus

I think of bedsheets not quite warm and momentarily open. Ready to receive. In spring and summer, lavender petals reveal stamens and stigmas approaching center flower. Leaves hold drylight near the bloom. Whose willingness, all gentle, forms an aura cloistering whatever we project. Softer than velour, a roselight of clear weather.

Coulter Hibiscus

Petals seem to have been laundered wash and wear, then draped across a hanger to relax into the smoothness. Eyes are drawn to gold red center that bleeds color mixed with sunlight into lower rays. Looks raw. Replaces the impression of virginity with purity in age. When wind comes, petals lightly separate the overlay, cream folded against cream.

Spring Evening Primrose

Moths with supple tongues reach into centers of the night blooms that appear before last frost. Pollen adheres in threads to moths, is carried plant to plant. At dawn, each blossom closes to the brush of light across still semaphore to night. Aloof or shy in code that asks continuance and peace during the light.

Engelmann Prickly Pear

Voluptuous bright yellow blooms embody our desire, erupt from poison pads with spines to which the javelina are immune. Life forms contain their possibilities and ruggedly survive (transcend). Evolve toward numbing fear. The prickly pear, a source of color, food, routinely flowers in spring these yellows that turn peach, these stamens that recoil when touched. (Bees, dusted past their burrowing.) Wine colored fruit ripens late summer, feeds coyotes, packrats, or is sweetened into jelly that extends by virtuosity our common understanding.

Desert Mariposa

Wild lily of desire infrequently appears. Bulb pushes the earth open, pressures daylight to receive vermillion. Centered gland anchors the smooth pressed flower. (Have I in mind the right rainfall and warmth, level of comfort with the slopes that spawn a tantalizing bloom.) Do I touch unscented cloth with lips that learn infinity, pure moment carried to a poised light patiently in love.

Fremont Pincushion

The closest moment to a desert snow seems punctuation that distills a backdrop into mercy or neglect. We have been close in mind so silver an array of hinges oiled and sweet. So anything could be let in. To care visibly is trespass. When I do so white shows on its stems. Not fleece brushed away. The long division where the deity evaporates at noon. Birds amid handfuls of seed lightning. Touch for which we had prepared or persevered with parts of tongues.

from

A Clove of Gender

from Section IV.

Literal Ponds

literal ponds (littoral ponds (lit

ponds soak la nuit with machinations till I'm

drowsy as a left looks in the latter moments of the harvest

when a crooning lifts the shade awhile (some

rusted sieve

discerns a Marxist from repeat dreams (wants to

klept something emotional because economic thought

is glued to freedom now when we are listening

(the detachment softly crazes its new (verifies

duplex mentality (shields doctors, lawyers

from sullen underthings found clinging to the bodies in the

street (allies' fecundity a simple

pasture quelled of its uniqueness (notice

voyages are young (they fray some lenses

of their clarity (a less determined quantity than

string erupted by a candle (many tastes of composition (stricture trace (by hand dear genius

perspicacity entranced by certain

tulip ferns   no, love (with extra

mind lingers on wording so

connect limps recent explanation

well like(d) salvo bleat

ozonic seeking (mystery

Dear _____, I'm sorry about force's being

equal to attraction,

iced with recovery (slim

punitive (realm of express

your paying job starts (Tuesday) to mean

everything not anything really at all

earth hitherto repudiates most ibid strings

(valence incalculable Voltaire defined as he Voltaire would

whim the thoughts to be (more probable than things

disposable appearing flowers linger in the mind

rotogravure would pension little pieces

into reasonable silence with a mention of

the signified (good taste) fraction (known

for some time slanted toward all mammals that endure us

and our smoke our weevils our tetrameter

a method or a weave of hope to grind out

repetition coated with preambular logic

(nails its head to hit unfolded

as desire relinquishes its hush

hush hope chest Polaroids for now

trembling in concert with

the tripod nest instead of camera

at its apex where we focus and deter

the grace notes from recurring

sans denouement easily a headstrong season

literature fathoms bar codes (to intrude upon

my thinking (milk cows in the sold field anymore

a property to hatch

or veer left (property to escalate

(to consecrate the vote into a law

what I am thinking now is Hindemith's music for use

and how she moved her hands when she said that

said this (he would nod

and she would stop whatever kneeling she had

contemplated and look up over across and hear him

consecrate his living to a sacrament (her

edification would seem by comparison

a frost-laden correspondence course assignment

he had graded with the best although not clearest

intentions (wool hats make fools warm also

identify some of the inklings (first, foremost (integrity

"train paintings to lie still and practice being

female" (what he said was Kurds are dying in the nectar wind

(suppose critics enjoyed you

features of the record entertained though portions were

of course scratched as with any passage of the decades

and enthusiasm whittling synthesis into some sort of

dyad I suppose toward decomposing every hair into

a finely knitted postum of a dry appearing day

(first draft becomes a child   the child decides

to narrate

(yesterday here is what happened   they removed

the seeds of the electricity   I happened to come down

with Marge (though didn't like her

after all she culprited my vision of the teaching role

a personality of glimmer or perceptual no virtual

centrality this way forward to a coast called anymoon

romance glistens comparable worth as in

identical threads (judgment and reflection

not to be confused with ambidextrous paint-

by-breath analogies and caves

in which subordinate species mime

what we are thinking (our concerns

fret like stringed models of

la langue and happiness the usual

predictable revolution meaning butterflies

and oranges and germs methodological

in kind the operation purely detour for the recency

in flowers who pertain most lunchly breach

birth (something proprioceptive

lurking in the aisles concluding whimsical and

sturdy and imaginative consent to trees strewn

across mind an elementary blue seeming condominium

the Sunday roast

ovened a short walk from the sacristy

(what weaves holiness and flesh

(bless, Father, each

orchestration consummately puissant

(heterogeneity

she calls me, leaves

voice mail about some things I've not forgotten

and will not (I don't want ever

to conform to her

delirium, posted elastic shipwrecked

fleur-de-lis and so forth till I am in part

crazed, craving mercy sandwiches (forgive

this camera framed (to look in on

itself the way we do the way we

perfectly absolve our sins and our blood chemistries

nothing, rich and ripe

(blancmange

yeasts toward eternal rendezvous

the boiling point (a cursive truth

spliced nocturne

brevity (a linear appearing sacrament

(gray wigs

obsess (hear fractions turn postcards

rondeau poached loosely in sea pan

(to make a living we succumb then

we succumb then we succumb (to layers indivisible

from shaken wheat from tallow and from

resin lifting this light bow in unison

with temperature most privacy

political in fact the coated snow

rebellion or the iron charm (the simmering rebellion

from

A Clove of Gender

from Section V.

How Partial Therefore Lovely

This Margin

I do homespun. You do breast stroke. All the feasts that would be hypothetical arrange themselves along the feasts that would be hypothetical. Of houses, this, mystific skates and treelength fences. Want to be the mist of long enough away. That she was happy as a mouthprint. Napkin weighed what lipstick weighed. I thought to keep a relic but I changed. Ride waiting. And a carnival cement first run and dangerous. Sleeping with retractable belief systems. Adream with track shoes pulsing forward.

Charm school, work clothes of natural fabric, a residual perfume

Weather Business

I fight off sleep with the same feist you can buy in hormone pellets at the hormone pellet store whose croutons make mush of otherwise compatible new minds. Their bony license plates have nicknames like *Jorge* or *Petrullus*, never *Winter*. One of the anonymous new flecks of wind just snapped my face as in a duel-to-be. I was heroic in detaching my two feet from the pom poms with the same severity as priests who occupy the confessional cabinet with fervor around sin and more. The things we spill there open possibilities for deep sensation near the peak experience of sleep. For twelve years I have slept beside you clutching the remote control in hopes of metaphorical variety. Here is how the human system lunges at its prey. It passes the examination on bureaucracy and brags about resultant fluency. A kind of epidemic in the world so crafted as to be revered. The way priest's robes...

Advice pool like a careful pond, remainders left to locate their own seasonings

Each Other's Line of Breath

Exactly as you say open my heartlight. Fall in love (the ripple sanctity undress as mention leaves harm's passageway. Fault line's brief sacrament. Here is how desire for touch...leaves out the whispering behind a graceful shore. So much the recently immaculate. As we were thinking recency and cloud. As we were instruments, each other's line of breath. Heart quenches what is birthed, expected to give thanks is equally a ritual. Of yet peace as would be learned. In context of the pretty skin. Would you like sacrament (where is the nexus of a sacrifice. I love the perfectly earned light without preface of cost. Relax those lovely shoulders as my hands describe a way.

Wildness, the darkest chamber of a heart that hears the horses with each water and concurrent pulse

Eros

Word choice elapses (what is in your eyes). The longing for red rock, magnetic field, as darkness slips into the lovely anonymity of daylight. Thought of touch recalls from dream a ripe, intentioned kiss. The path of an equation, feminine (already there). Silk moves in answer to a wind desired.

Delicious snailspeed, time to savor what will be

When Clouds, Class Clown

Loose change gangs up on zeal the way we porch ourselves. The way we lawn up out-of-reach recurring furniture farm teaming around likely planets. Wield knobs and carte blanche episodes. Spectrum encompassing the bland and wild. Minus nearby cusp.

Supportive streetnoise, tendencies, the wish to shift diameters

from

A Clove of Gender

from Section VI.

For Leisure, Boundaries

Come Harvard me, surround

Most flexibly this body with your heart

In mind, I lust for

Comprehension that resembles leaves

Deliriously falling in the proper places

At the proper time keepsakes momentum us alive

Just Zen enough a sacrament

Of let these muscles glow

After a climb, each lovely superstition

Places faith in speech and faith in touch

The luminosity of several windows

Pointed toward daydream erasible

As feeling slithers from a habit system

Into indentations ledged by

All of the raised places

Happiness affords

for leisure, boundaries compare themselves to white

a cage sends messages (forms other

cages press my life, a text is said

immersed in the reflected genericity

presumed apart from passion's

sole luciferic depth and height,

immersion (take the trouble to appear

formidable to all endearments, suddenly snow

cusps moist with solid white,

sheer curtains padded into cubes

upper Pacific limelight

shield of mercy (this, exactly how far

I will go with hands, though not with mind

alight, eternity's position statement

on the sacred dream, a resonant delay

sort of astounding, picnic shaped, time-bound (almighty

pallor, chipt paint sacristy (enough

blue wine May-

flower heresy all mine sequest

gemline around the oval roses

port (the verb-noun

glowing simple as sludge would

in another life held fast

the chemistry is marred from happening to worlds

he is deterior in sandwage

chips 'coil near the edge of

scores for fun Sheherezade

sometimes almost awake the matters of this world

climb home to dustworthy polite lives

situated hereby in a matter of these months go by

to harvest viol

Miranda she was poor a parrot (glum sometimes

what about her ego frosts (my ego

slumbers in her presence, winks

and drains its bladder inconspicuously thus

gracefully I think of nothing but baked weather

in the seamless park, the lateral park,

my stocking feet after the morning climb,

the likely sequence of long meetings about nothing

the creation of the minutes to reflect the proper

form of nothing, a series of statements

designed to make the majority feel better

about wasted time, perhaps not wasted,

from here atop the peak I can see smoke around buildings

haze over the roadways, and a flume of melody

that hypothetically would move with care,

transgress to blaze of chords unwanted and unrhythmic,

even at a distance (self-announcing

from

A Clove of Gender

from Section VII.

Wind Topography

I'm talking in your sleep again

(the airplane aisle, a gulf preceding

avid blue, tormented, regional-appearing,

undermines (seepage rinsed by

lift, the stub of wings-go-limber

in the mind, points artificial (focus

so involved, the thought of evolution

nurtures every light, a limit to

finesse as we envision sprawling

worth of the soprano who redeems

the core beneath *spin* on an aria

subtle not especially

amazed yet (mouth I watch ajar

whose energy delineates

more petals of the flowers

dyed an artificial blue

a lexicon abbreviating (silk of love is how

breath safens toward indulgence

manger tepid, clumsy looking episodes

deep into highways

the pitch of health sales

flaxen loft of grain so

periodic snare drums enter into

shapely dreams repeatable the moment after

pencilling the lead time and

a graceful personality to bear on

fortunata rings steepled,

homogenized entirely

(rituals seep into the least thinking

safely we connive their consequence

formal, informal versus etcetera

(abandonment fails to emit the certain sacrament

connectedly we sing minus a reason (for the trees, offspring, perennial

indulgence (formulae divert diversity (the *yonge sonne*

awash blue certain (noticed she took care of things,

ideas chastened the cement (manner of speaking

sentences the garden to be toolfast (process of emissions testing

loosens timeline to a metronome with melody and light

ontology goat-scented (reason siphons

prescient elements in mind, intrusive factions

introduce unstructured wind (soft cloth ferrets induction

light, opacity, demonstrable

clue lenses capture or release name

repetition pounces after hours

we say we breeze through understanding

(grasp reports to being who we are now

(*meaningful objectives* topple why we're here

salt pellets on the road (a pleasure, mission-driven

expertise seems *floundering*, face first into

the levity of merchandise aglow with

heavelength a result of head-

to-head something (connective divot surreptitious

mention, we're surprised (often

"for those of you unfamiliar with the Dallas-Fort Worth

Airport..." space of a few minutes

Cleveland C-3, Columbus, C-9, Detroit C-6, Fort Myers C-12, etc.

how we learn

our suppositions (well in hand

the algorithmic thrust of most held temperature

another theory frequently espoused has leisure

glibly in the wake of sliver mention

although sparse it trickles, although everything

indulgent is acquired, the several beaches, mercy

bench press white water happiness, again adrift

New Poems:

Previously uncollected; originally appeared in the following magazines:

Phoebe, Grist-on-Line, Ribot, Big Scream, Kiosk, First Intensity, Lost and Found Times, Intuit, Dirigible, The Alterran Poetry Assemblage, Dadababy

Gorecki in July

"We do not communicate. We signal."

- *Edmund Jabes*

All we wanted was subjectively to stay home among probable weeds and close the blinds.

Again she called from what we feelingly describe as her darkness but mostly it is spatial.

The ascending tones within melodic minor make sense in the way of tension furnished place none of the pieces match.

Methodology is of course the study of method but is used to mean method while the fear is method doesn't have an engineering feel.

She heard sounds piled on sounds accepted offer either close the door or turn it off (shared moments deceive us pleasantly.

The ceiling fan perfectly tortures those preferring stillness (It is hard to talk to a soprano for the same reason.

A saddle seems extraneous to horses mostly not to persons who weave blankets.

Career is a spittoon positioned where the safety likes to splinter from the shelter family in language.

Mild dosages are paper animated prayers crafted to look natural floating in irrigation southerly.

A sculpture ruse sprinkled with heat placemats the silver has-been hospitality (no longer love you).

Snapshots lack capacity of taffy. Leave them their moment spousal as dusk.

Midwestern underwear signs from the line often confused with drawing board in two dimensions.

Leaflets, then, arranged to seem orchid colored gladiola she would buy in crispy paper at a corner shop on volume.

Paraphrase hurts with inexactness leaving the lips, received, a reinvented posture from first motion dance (hunger especially.

Theology, a patently unclear looking elbow, the intent of this retreat, these swans, pale swans especially accustomed to nothing we're accustomed to.

I saw them often in the small and stuttering Greek restaurant without their seeing me, when I would take out food, wondered knowing perfectly the way it feels to talk back to dementia.

The seagulls, mist below them, sound, my footprints and the waves in uniform, unrecognizable and perfectly recognizable.

Thales

I like the Upper Peninsula because some of it is wet. And when it's not it's frozen you can glide all over it in frigid uninhibited though asexual movement (unwatched). It really is a mitten town up there all salt along the cleavage of a highway rotting Fords while new. You skate past debts and safety. Usually the thing that makes you stay is birth. So if you visit you are halfway liked when they do not remember when you came. Neglect to borrow sugar once and you are likely in. Two quarts of something to go under the hood. You can look out all right at Lakes Michigan or Superior and think of frozen fishes. To be held in abeyance is not the same as being held. A mother reputed to like domesticity aligns herself with wine. With just enough salt to assuage a fraction of the grief. Look at the shrill ice coming to a point and listen to the foghorn brave this temperature when nothing could be passing anywhere.

She's Lovely on Prozac

She's lovely on Prozac, how I wish she had been born with it. Her hairdo softened and small socks pastel her tanned legs so. I'm pretty, simply looking there. It isn't dark, my milestones earnest-money all caress in mood stability with tie tacks pinching every solo ritual. We would enjoy what food was warm while we were talking. It was not infrequent to be likable. We matched again. Her inner situation comedy retracted harsh bones in the ordered fish and soup that came with it. What's marked about a play day, patterned lace and kindling to assort the choice of candles. Anyway, the fog I prayed would never lift did not lift in our lifetime. When she touches into being a harmonic, fresh-cut flowers quaff a stripe of water in the skinny vase. A moisture to be added to her pre-existing smiles.

Iff

almost the sleevetip of October
partial to a fire
I look from cold to opposite
repair, the licensure all coded
so my handprint is
like anybody else in me
the cozy furniture undresses
mood on mood it is not practical
to bakesale any reverie intact
in two in moments teachward
so we're sampling a hypotenuse
while listening to a forecast
be the day itself

❈   ❈   ❈   ❈   ❈   ❈

Dear S_____,

Look at all of these protracted daisies. Even as early as this night is, think. A trouncing hemline soft where winkmarks are. Rinsed death furnaces along a window ledge. Fraternal syllables encode a syllabus quaint partly reachable. How did I do, pointwise, with your percussive heart. Its glove fit, my heroics. Spurty radio with entertainment funning down the chin. The many loaves of heaven are inaccurate. Equality explicitly could be citrus left on trees. I mean aside from polar temperatures inside you. Mussable as beetroot summer. What things once sorted remain parallel. Remember averages mean nothing. When a robin isn't close to home nearbrained where endpoints have been harvested. How many monies tax free leak from pocket thumbs how few remaining moods are spooled across the rest. The husbandry it takes to be political is climbing out the window of a

nervous system. Granular, it loosens some of custom and
redemptive lungs the height of rowdy, round, and punctual
hysteria.

❋   ❋   ❋   ❋   ❋   ❋

grimly feedled so
the little birds unlift incentive toward
suburbia hand-carved
unnattily presented mild St. Francis
holding in his hands some food for birds,
birds fully ambulatory
winged also stand rapt
become delicious for someone
St. Francis his own halo
offers and receives
the thought of sleep contains
insomnia so beautiful a pie could be
no more than wilderness
as guessive as the full court press
of clock, appropriate rubbed lamp
so something learns to happen,
of course happens

❋   ❋   ❋   ❋   ❋   ❋

6:40 a.m., our guests about to be departing
I go foraging
this mild way
toward the leavings of once
civilized convention
just one
waitress (not server)
opens Nosh-a-Rye
I barely think
to order six

copies of bagel in various
and four decaf to go
in comfort hers
all little of my world is
shining

❊   ❊   ❊   ❊   ❊   ❊

she reported how to Marriott away the weekend
primer lacked some of the needed silk
to thumbs down migraines on the stove front
miles per hour uncalculated
ask guardian angels to lunch
amend what you were saying to the rodeo
when hands shook open and released
a possum kind of love topped seventy degrees ok sixty
sufficient time to board space
while coughing up a siphoned shame
eggs timed properly would list a little to the right
and so with hampers white in laundry costs and task-related
beestings
when you see success what do you mean
Catholicism of course lingers

❊   ❊   ❊   ❊   ❊   ❊

soft plant
teaches origin
light shock
value
lapsed
shared
values

❊   ❊   ❊   ❊   ❊   ❊

Dear S_____,

she was my customer
my tietack, friended crapshoot,
puck along white silver skated highway
yarned before the stop sign twin aged
demiurge next door to purgative incentless
battery some judge must
wade through, praxonyms
resuscitate the twiddling hosts of thumbs
hurting from recent handsprings
now mossed over

❊   ❊   ❊   ❊   ❊   ❊

plaudits

halfway to Costa Mesa

plea barg-

anastonish

coy bilge zoom lensed

patriectomy

peacepipe white wood

waist high then

home basked (appreciably)

❊   ❊   ❊   ❊   ❊   ❊

she is invited but would rather "snuggle in" beside temptation "just a splash"
feels inconvenienced by the square-shaped hospitality
would prefer to cauterize the present tense with past barbed wire
prove she plays an instrument and loves the instrument more than her idleness
expects response to her dissatisfaction about idleness

((and drug rough plie
   sandwiches the ralston
   and the heat weaves
   timed for exotic
   wheeze so bronzed

to frame and all the does-this-mean dry ice
so blame slides down the surf
plant thus unevenly   (provides)
would you do this at home
(yes/no) approach and so forth

❊   ❊   ❊   ❊   ❊   ❊

Warm till sweet the latest ice. Wish frost to part a little red this *yonge sonne*. Verity beside the lace wheeze. Off-white cleavage early champion (off temp also freezing wide with lemmings salt the framed lined wide lineage half open. Orangely we walk the counseling walk. Erase turmoil this much. Huevos kayak red bandana-ed boom box. Slow and murky is not true of swine. Whole river (sections) tributaries want to have us like them. Only guide, is she half charming. White shirt until we are the river. Are we (thus) river or sun. Do you go diving. Blood supposedly attracts. My brother. Surfers wearing black suits wet and slick how can uncanny be. To think so. Pretty siftless. Change the subject and the petty theft of karma. Yes a rare and not. Unusual enough to seem dense as limitless. The preface "happy" before holiday what does it mean to be retired. Gray personality. Weak lacking in intensity. Wolf down the gemosphere. A waiting room is beautiful nothing to do. Linoleum with scattered hair. Pale message accidentally sketched on the floor. Define outrage. Dust over carpeting. To pour five after. Laminate and trial piece. The after page and several wall hangings. Hardware soft. Moist hardware sponge. What next to touch. Refine community. A ream of swift new white papel. Hello igloo. Hello intact. Refusing to come down (with something).

❄   ❄   ❄   ❄   ❄   ❄

Titles of Prayers

Prayer for Female Olive Tree
Prayer for Several Fractions
Prayer for Keepsakes
Prayer for Clients
Prayer for Old Brick
Prayer for the Computer
Prayer for Tilted Sidewalks
Prayer for Oak Leaves Falling
Prayer for Fear
Prayer for Chosen Family
Prayer for Sweet Flute Breath
Prayer for Abundance
Prayer for Hyphenation as a Form of Individuality
Prayer for Police
Prayer for Catcher's Mask
Prayer for Partner
Prayer for White Rice Cereal
Prayer for Patio Enclosed

Prayer for Practice
Prayer for Oil Paintings
Prayer for the Bassoon to Quiet Down
Prayer for Carpet
Prayer for Bedtime
Prayer for Companionship
Prayer for Walls
Prayer for Instrument
Prayer for Linkage in Space
Prayer for Red Clay Mountain
Prayer for the Not Stray Emotions

❊   ❊   ❊   ❊   ❊   ❊

She excuses how he is. She's running him for office he's not running for. She's running for acceptance in a marathon including everybody else. She will distract them in her mind from weighing her. She will appoint him king. She will unravel common sense and wrestle it to the earth. She does not ask them to befriend him. She acquires Exhibit A and shapes him in the image of her need. A brother in possession of the weapon he won't use. Who would protect her and protect them in her name. She hears herself declare him tender. Kisses just the friendship they have had. Then speaks of it. He listens to the others tell her stories back. The ones who know she does not know they talk to him from levels other than... Who do not need to worship with a fraction of themselves. Who do not need her sentences to like him but won't love him to the level that she does. Who will not flinch. Who will not suffocate the common sense that loves and keeps them quiet and protected past her love.

❊   ❊   ❊   ❊   ❊   ❊

structure causes early weeds to be thought
beautiful again, again mellifluous appearing
former seeds most likely to succeed
the willow simplifies and afternoon a fan rotating
toward delinquent shorelines windless
patch the missing places in a life with life
and forge the signature of maker
how a thing is shaped illumines
how a thing is shaping other things
emotions for example mutually color, flavor, and
erase promotional materials from space
the way we're used to feeling
most of the advantage sings to sleep experience
our wide open enough plain conforms
to first glimpses into pater noster and such
prayers of envy, prayers of pride
and diseconomy as simple as the web
incinerated by this sudden look of prayer
before the spider is transformed beyond its handiwork

❉   ❉   ❉   ❉   ❉   ❉

as the piece of trees are wine

        yes plant
        oval wide
        don't use the words
        breath, light, flower
        draw (instead) freehand the
        tonal canvas
        rhubarb in Menominee
        finger around
        the lips
        think of an error

             (arrow)
             margin
             (shirts)

   ✼   ✼   ✼   ✼   ✼   ✼   ✼

my father's grave
opines close
to sea water favoring
the salt to partial
freshness partial clarity
all people in resemblance
tool chest their way past
siphoned wind
march painted prim at cost
melinda was her name
scratched out on velvet
I tell you what
that cost

   ✼   ✼   ✼   ✼   ✼   ✼   ✼

Slumber parties each break up

At last anonymous

For winter ask

Whose siphonage now bedded down

Anoints this caliber

Of down time "field"

Meaning some sacrament

Eventually resumes

Meaning the silver now belonging

To the children will be
Put away for now

And polished when these hands

Release moments the body

Of this memory as thick

Now feastless held, elapsed

From holiday to blankness

First thought no gift

Then reconsidered

Pure

❋   ❋   ❋   ❋   ❋   ❋

much of shape shift oval circumstance relax

forebears punk rock forwardly adrift points

same dead harbor (more practicum than

undressive worth bayberry likenesses share draft

parts of slippage silver (loneliness

defects infects reflects you (cardboard milk

prelaxes how you often are (I'm talking silkfront

screams of acreage new as
glossolalia imported from the south of France or some

refractive mountain of the sugar pints

just droll is how we're thinking unanimity

portion control and track shoes to the left of

silt from the Alaskan field garage

jauntily minced with screen tabs also

worked unduly hard pressed (flowers look especially

nice dried the arrangement of them plentiful

filed gracetones modest in their harbor

usually plumable

on card stock as photos happen

always to be sudden for (intact

❊   ❊   ❊   ❊   ❊   ❊

Chant

Furled new whitened episodes elapse until white stones of us attract some moss sheet rock plantain. Remarkable new curfews sentence us to hip deep death. In-style and perishable norms accommodate big bad epoxy living past its use. Utility is browned in butter left unspoken as the trill attracts first sacredness. The only mud we're left with hopes us down the floor. And modifiers change the temperature of usually clear norms having sentences to ride in. If a horoscope reads like suspicion fry it in predominant erasive weather. If each succulent depicted in the book has shaped itself around the town, remunerate at will in conscience. It was not fun to leave the country on a horse of any kind. A frail young collie also you could watch track in the dirt from pastures. Or a moth reserved for streetlights mimicking just moon's broad field of light. Think how fear is a denominator again. There's no describing any of the words just right. No mood that ever matches. No economies of scale that make resistance right under this circumstance.

Sleeves worn inside out, probable growth, pencils we call mechanical

❊ ❊ ❊ ❊ ❊ ❊

piece together

one and then

another of this (skyside

perch involved

the lights

equal

tact-

fabric mountain strong

and mountain

thought of mountain

Remarkable Attention

Past midnight, conversation unsavors the least sum of modest squares. Epitomes thumb their way home. If work were not prerequisite, I'd drive a cobbled, harness-free, indigenous rattle T for trap; I'd hide you in the rumble seat; I'd court you fervently; record the lack of my successes...Entre nous, this bijou of a best bet falsifies investment opportunities connected to this free range chicken room. You might undress your elves and find their pulse points not unlike our own. You might as likely reinvent card catalogues or retrieve the fruit cake rounding corners of the withering half blue unsalted friendships. Sodium measures lack of will. Imprints the thriving positives so we can read them, entertain suspicion, crop the photos where we can still read our sugared faces. Part of the inspection of eternity occurs based on the elbow grease applied to routine tasks. And how they glow like inexpensive watches shining past the point of logic after stores have let them go to wrists. Remarkable attention has been paid to most mature appearing adjectives. When we are slow we dive bomb our enabling laxity to earn these pre-included sheep. Swatches of anonymous field clover fails to pierce the horizontal mainframe of viewfinder. Philosophy has undergirded all we love. A catalogue of the sopranos foregrounds who we are and how we know. First person starts describe anatomy until the engine loses steam and ground. A fortune ready to be made unclasps its will for hours. Many of the same detentions come to me when it is willowy long past the hour of midnight when the conversation sleeps itself to interest bearing homilies.

Tooting one's own horn, locating audience, affectioning resultant newborn conversation

Isosceles Relationships

She was watering the hubcaps when I met her. Evolution tires of us. So suit yourself about arresting the impending freight train. Chemistry becomes our issue. Veto power belongs in the third column. Perfect love requires a prior hatred. When will we go back to kissing our TV and pressing it the way we like. Surmise for me why chemistry must be returned to the beholder. Summarize what you would like to have assigned. If I facilitate have I contributed. And what derives from what across team looking class. The bottleneck is often capable. The bottleneck only as rigid as the dirt. Each sentence mouthed until we're quiet as a corporate seal. Myopic vehicles perform for the hot air balloons the chase. Attrition hampers style. Remain in your position until graves remind us to be docked. Take any lead you see emerging. Handle emptiness by filling spaces as so many crossword squares. This is my manifesto this is not. Erase my mood when you are free. I saw he should be crying but was wrinkling metal as presumably a substitute. Whatever you have said will become Kosher the result of culture's streaming through the wood. The force behind my questions pressures a presumed containment. Isosceles relationships stay wan. A sweater not corrupt may still warm. Customers become our night our morning our contentment. Say what you've prepared and own it. Wear a shirt perspire all over it then let it go. The vacuum Helen uses is industrial plus plus. With this ring I thee...simplify the Godhead. We serve ourselves we document we long term what we often try. My strong suit is to communicate when wanted and before. Internal policy is half good. We'll improve when we're prepared. Pasta as fuel burned cleverly or minus noticeable adverbs. Most to the point how accurate was her response how naturally offered.

A Mood Apart from Singing Charles Ives

What if I never awoke tin metal yellow in braids broken on
the telephone this dervish voice I never spooned into my
Perry Mason glyph and toke and jest and shuck 'n jive
momentum thus and fairy cakes the lumber stiffens softens
gives way to the tuberous redundancy amuck run episodic
thumbs crickets Purina spots my moist pen what we fear
incents meticulous disturbances are Virgo spinlight mention
the anonymous protect from mental jungles ease comes fresh
a mood apart from singing Charles Ives in the family
room the expression in a coat the pull the elocution like a
dance committee voice does what yes eloquence snakes in
water plenty rims to beautiful away apart from stench too
near the roses perpendicular apart zone slander come to
chemical dependency silk parts the water reasonable silk
peacefully within tree houses panting the plantation mountain
kiss the able centipedes rum weathered in a hoop the shape-
less house lacking direction slice of pie I use my favorite pen
again the legislative session burns bicuspid holes into my
pockets storms are infidels with too good looking daughters

Wild Yam

Picturesque makes points like these: enough of them and you'll be tidy till the nevermore of patent leather prides its way through dark feats laborious and not your own. How does humming sound when solipsistic vehicles belonging to your osprey make a hard left and you're being pickpocketed for the third time this trimester. Blue carves shuttle weather near the slaving pierce of rooms. Entirely trademarked wheat germ strangles every gentleman remaining in the path of coastal tongues with power to unthatch what we are hurting to be thinking. Reminiscent thought hangs heavy on a divan pointed to the heft of solid brawn. You make your own lampshades your way of watering the lawn and reminiscing. When I hear her steps I then conjecture she must be approximately home. Who might be there to offer traffic signals to the dearly departed if that is what they are. I like a dull man at a party possibly to stabilize. That's when I am about to mention the bewitching motions to the judge who for the past ten minutes looks as though she's not meant to have heard anything I've said.

The Tonsure Cure (Lui-Meme)

nest night pictifies my until volubly also a peach and mighty fling screen pulse attached. go green skilled pasteurized we while awaying clone our breathing. yesibels are true and slur to wheat this mindful alsoing. now pondered summer sure. etruscan for the mo. we 'lectrify willpoints as cured as roseate true samurai. go windowy as little warlock solvy yet. too true to have been tainted.

Abscondily With Plenty Mercredi

Kilt of snare prepped fluff until I trellised sakes from quelching volumosity so lawned it browed. So continence true floored wheezed back agon and tuliped lo and braveward. The kibosh went cool so rivery it wilded what I noshed. A bake sake quill pen chiseled diseconomy so cumbered where the crewel sunk whicherling unslankily to twirl and seasuch blousing curl whee windlorn omen klatsch. So bounded and implorish quizzing satch catess midnight obstreperie. The whill and prequence fathom in this mewn door sea salache and sarabande. Mown mildew in a kriss and patch. Abscondily with plenty mercredi in balance. Blanching to the tumor of neglect all ice warts keepsake as we bland nomadic forsworn ever lily pomp and gladio till ruck sack mid-course chanterelle we tweak and bandage and unbandage scores and fellow moths oil changily the Krugerrand aplombist shares slipped quid.

Frame

Amplitude convenes a kiss. Heredity blooms once fathers have laid claim. To the soprano wafflehood of aria maps dotted with downlinks. Shrill nests approach the precipice of stress. Commodities are heartfelt combs with swish in them. That clamor to be fortified with threats of their inclusion. Winter waits to foist surprise on shallow rakes besieged by future flurry. All the leaves cow down. We're mangers anymore. Threads anchor every space we have for follicles. As cloistered as the simpering full nest to match these tithes and shutters latched and forms of burgeoning...

Dividends

Spinet your little eyes out, go ahead and drizzle. Davenports once in the street are now moved in. Your off-the-shoulder attitude (directory assistance) can be seen to pry. Why don't you. The sole maternity I have is tired of me at last. Unclothe lyrics so I can disclaim their meaning. The qualming of guitar chords pounces without conscience. Mediocrity opens a fist that should be neighborly. Why she wore mustard I will never... Bathing in calendula is one thing; drying out, another. Legal pads seem fresh while they are being used. Rose, the color, opts to freshen light seaworthy. Champions, not bronzed until we name them.

Tapioca drilled by random silence, tease modality of shoulders

Subjects

How something looks from many angles might repeal acts previously uncommitted. Ripe angels slice a madrigal because *composed* means soil. Counterintuitive uplift of material to dust off *progressively*. Cease bones gin up the odometer of lust included in an index fund. Sliced buzzards ripple the anemia. "Sit down, Son. Your mother and I would like to talk to you." Eventually, the microphone leaks projection of intent. Prayer isn't wobbly to the hearer's mum. Fortunes reverse. Full spectrum reciprocity maims the continent. Witnesses leave home unannounced. Whose *something to do* reams passers by. "A piece of information" smarting in the diary. Stageproof as it comes, enormity spoons teachings. Propinquity tastes healthy, but is not. Historians shift kindling, choosing to warm hands instead of making acts. Pirouette seems chance sleep that turns out dreams with the consistency of down. Vicinities are only relative to loyalty and continuity. Extravagant as equal signs spattered about with too-low dosages of working conscience.

We Would be Sheep

We would be sheep along the mollycoddled highway
Any smart set absent from our novel lungs and thinking
Nobody but us is supple half enough
Nobody outside these walls talks honey soothingness

To match the how-I'm-planted-here-at-full-attention
For your mind and elbows, how I'm green
In your smooth light that fastens
My convictions to my suddenly abandoned heart

And headlong plunge into the beauty of the market
That is jumproped in our seasoned
Backstroke tandeming like twelve string
Handsome all these old ones we agree we've never heard

Because the ivy likes attention
And we're its scenery batch warmed
Filling shaken light enough
To parse a verb we'll happily collaborate on framing home

An Interview with
Sheila E. Murphy

An interview with Sheila E. Murphy

When did you begin writing and publishing seriously?

In the fall of 1978, just a couple of years following my relocation to Phoenix, the work began come together. There was no mystery as to why. A close friend, who knew that writing mattered more to me than any process, sat with me and helped me actually *complete* about eleven fragments that I had waiting to become poems. The initial impetus was that another friend in Michigan had told me of an opportunity to submit a chapbook somewhere. The editor was considering groupings of eleven poems. So my mentor and I chipped away at the activity until we had eleven pretty good ones. The chapbook opportunity never materialized. But the friend in Michigan suggested that I send to *Salt Lick,* Jim Haining's wonderful magazine. The word was, "Even if he doesn't take something, he'll send you baseball cards or other fun things." Well, I did send, and back came a note from Jim, saying "Like your work enough to print." The two he initially accepted (the list for that issue would be upped to five or seven, as I responded to his request for more — he didn't want to feature "snippets" of writers' work, but preferred to present a more complete picture of what was going on) were "Solipsism" and "The Mail," both still good ones, in my view. Well, naturally, a little positive reinforcement following some good direction launched me. I couldn't stop writing. The thing was, I'm sure I didn't know what I was doing then. I'm equally sure that we simply become more attuned to what we *might* be doing. But some of the early work for anyone who's serious may likely shine. It usually represents something just aching to "get out." Following that first acceptance, letter writing became increasingly important to me and played an important role in the writing process. I write to many writers and editors, some of whom have become my closest friends. And in many cases, I have never met these friends in person.

How has your writing changed over the years?

My writing started out being very accessible, often narrative and humorously descriptive. While I still try for that in some pieces, I've added some categories. For instance, much of my work has moved in innovative directions. The dance in language has become central to my play. I invent a lot of forms, adapt forms to help them sing me awake. I hear the syllables reform themselves. I let the forms become *containers* that accommodate the mind and heart so form is not a distracting obstacle to singing the perceptions. I've written whole books using a particular structure that I find for them. *Teth* (Chax Press, 1991), for instance, consists of 81 pages of text, each of which is comprised of 81 words. *Obeli: 21 Contemplations* (Pygmy Forest Press, 1992) consists of 21 poems, each of which is in 21 lines, 7 words per line. In *Tommy and Neil* (Sun/Gemini Press, 1993), actually two "books" in one volume, the section for my brother Tommy consists of 36 pages, each of which is comprised of three "patches" of words, having 54, 13, and G words, respectively. The book was a gift on his 36th birthday, 6/13/54. Thus, the word pattern, which helped me crystallize what I desired to make and share on that occasion. And I can't leave out the haibun (Japanese form consisting of a prose passage, followed by a single line haiku of variable syllables - "cousin of haiku," I call it). I have written a vast number of pieces in this form, as I found it highly compatible with my process. I first saw the form used in English in a 1984 issue of *Sulfur,* where John Ashbery wrote "Six Haibun." He'd apparently become familiar with the form from the anthology *From the Country of Eight Islands,* which I reviewed, finding the English translations of the Japanese masters fairly bland compared to Ashbery's vibrant and inventive use of this language. I was so taken with Ashbery's work in this vein that I wanted to "try one." By now I have seemingly reinvented the form for myself, and enjoy it immensely. I continue to try to do new things with my work. One recent addition is my collaboration with the Celtic Harpist Megha Morganfield. We've produced a cassette tape called *The Weight and Feel of Harps*. And we've performed together a great deal. My prose pieces based upon wildflowers of the desert South-west are the mainstay of this collection, which also includes a number of haibun. It happens that my voice and the plucked strings of the harp fuse together very well. The whole process is exciting. I write a number of portraits, as represented by a short collection called *Twelve Portraits of Beverly C,* as yet unpublished as a collection. I like to write single line poems, many of which Don Wentworth of *Lilliput Review* has seen fit to use. We're hoping to gather a collection of one-line pieces. I also write very long poems, such as "Small Beads of Torque" that came out in *Tyuonyi* (Santa Fe, New Mexico) a few years back. This piece alternates prose and lineated passages.

Describe your writing habits.

I do my writing in two ways: I have an Acer Aspire, an IBM Think Pad 360 (a gift from my mother) and I have many pens, along with bundles of yellow and white legal pads that I acquire at office warehouse sales. I either pour out writing directly onto the keyboard or I use the right pen and paper for the portable occasion and just let go. I love to be alone when I write, although I've perfected the practice of writing during conferences. I sit in the lecture hall and listen while I write, often integrating spoken lines from the speaker into my text. Some years ago, I had the misfortune of having to attend defensive driving school, as I'd made a U-turn (legal in Arizona) in front of the main Post Office at Van Buren (where it is *not* legal!) during one of my nightly mail drops (Things go out as late as 10:00 p.m., and I'm obsessed with getting things into the mail!). Well, this scrubbed looking cop came along and stopped me, and I wound up choosing to go to driving school (not the first time: I also tend to have a lead foot, so I've attended class on at least two other occasions). During the class, I held my practiced pose of attentiveness, nodding, smiling, occasionally raising my hand, all while composing poems. One of the pieces, entitled "8/6/94" was accepted for publication shortly after the incident. On airplanes, I write a great deal. And at home, I sometimes create in my office, or propped up in bed. One of my favorite places to write in on the back patio, where it's hot and peaceful. 1 like to write every day, but sometimes that's not workable. I gauge my output by month, tracking rather carefully what has emerged. That usually involves several reasonably good days of writing. I'm naturally a night person, but find the quietest parts of the day (in either direction) to be best.

What are you thinking about with respect to your writing these days?

I seem constantly to grapple with abstraction versus accessibility in my work. The way that I've chiefly resolved this issue (again and again!) is to do many types of writing. My life is filled with "double majors." This pattern began in college, and has continued in any number of ways. Among the ways is the enjoyable division between my writing life and my business life. Another way is certainly in the kinds of writing that I do. Some work moves off into "ever ever" land, whereas some is very recognizable. On the spectrum of expectation and surprise, I far prefer surprise. I call some narrative/descriptive writing "pitiful papa on the front porch" writing, meaning all too predictable and *not new*. Regardless of the place a text may occupy on the aforementioned spectrum, it is the language and the sound that fascinate me and remain with me long after reading or hearing a work.

How do musical and visual art forms f figure into your writing?

I am a trained flutist, having played and performed since age 10. Even when the vocabulary of music is not evident in my poems (and it often is), the texture of the work resembles music. That is not n conscious intention, although I generally prefer language that works well *as music*. I write for the ear, and language is music to me. I listen all the time to conversation, to natural and to city sounds. I hear them as music. I love accents in speech, and love to mimic them in an appreciative way. Over the past several years, I have cultivated a taste for visual art that did not come to me at birth, as did the music. On display in my home are some wonderful works by such visual artists as Rupert Loydell, Linda Bryant, Linda Mundwiler, Cynthia Miller, David Chorlton, and Harper Leah. In recent years, I have written in response to visual art with great pleasure, both as an individual effort, and in collaboration with Beverly Carver. One of the pieces I did individually in response to a contemporary sculptural piece can be found in the first volume of *The Gertrude Stein Awards in Innovative Poetry,* edited by Douglas Messerli. A collaborative work done with Bev Carver in response to an interesting aleatoric sculpture appears in an issue of *Central Park*. In the current issue of *Stride,* works of mine created in response to visual images by Rupert Loydell are included. This particular exploration has been satisfying, as I "hear" a number of discoveries by looking at Rupert's work.

What part does geography, specifically the landscape of the Southwestern United States, play in your writing? Although I never would have expected to feel this way before moving to the Southwestern United States about 20 years ago, the landscape here strongly influences my perceptions and my work. In my view, psychic geography makes great intuitive sense. I truly have found my place in Phoenix, Arizona. The red mountains (The name of my street is "Monterosa" meaning, literally, "red mountain") accept light in a way that can compare to nothing else. One learns the seasons here by fragrance, rather than by obvious startling changes, such as those in "snow country." Blossoms in the desert air create an incomparable perfume. It takes most new residents here a good long time to learn to see the beauty in the desert. For many people, greenery equates to beauty. The "brownery" and tan hues we have here do not look beautiful to some people. I don't even remember exactly what I used to think about the physical appearance of this place. All I know is that it's glorious to me now, and that I love it. To the specific question, I would say that Phoenix, Arizona offers everything that I could want: a private kind of desert place that is also the seventh most populous city in the United States. One collection that is forthcoming from a press in Tucson, Arizona is called *Heat a Form of Privacy Like Snow.* When it is extremely hot in the desert in summer, the feeling resembles that after a snowfall. Quiet is pervasive. For a number of years, I climbed a mountain, Squaw Peak, located not too far from my home, each morning. This helped me attune to the desert, which is the most prayer-like of any physical place that I can name.

You are known to be a prolific writer. How important is this to your composition process?

For me, writing needs to be a constant and ongoing event that is built into the process of living. I have found that writers tend to appear on a spectrum somewhere between writing constantly/producing numerous poems and writing extremely infrequently/producing very few poems. I fall on the abundant end of that spectrum. It's important to me to produce a great deal. (An artist friend of mine calls me a "produce-aholic" - very different from a workaholic!) I believe that the key issue connected to this is momentum. I need to build the momentum and fluency that facilitate my operating on a vibrational frequency that suits the expectations and desires I have for writing. It's probably important to add here that writers have individual working patterns and styles, and that it's best to follow what works for oneself. I know writers who craft a line, think about that line, and completely remake that line before moving on to the next one. And other individuals see fit to pour out writing of all sorts on a daily basis. Neither extreme is correct or incorrect. It's just a matter of creating something that fits an individual's own temperament and style of working.

Composed in 1994 and 1996.

Parts of this interview first appeared in *Abbey* magazine, 1994.

Potes & Poets Press Publications

Bruce Andrews, *Executive Summary,* $9.00
Dennis Barone, *Echoes,* $14.00
Dennis Barone, *Forms / Froms,* $7.00
D. Barone / P. Ganick, *The Art of Practice: 45 Contemporary Poets,* $18.00
Martine Bellen, *Places People Dare Not Enter,* $8.00
Steve Benson, *Reverse Order,* $9.00
Paul Buck, *no title,* $8.00
O. Cadiot / C. Bernstein, *Red, Green & Black,* $8.00
Abigail Child, *A Motive for Mayhem,* $8.50
A. Clarke / R. Sheppard, eds., *Floating Capital,* $12.00
Norma Cole, *Contrafact,* $10.50
Norma Cole, *Metamorphopsia,* $8.50
Cid Corman, *Root Song,* $7.50
Beverly Dahlen, *A Reading (11-17),* $8.50
Tina Darragh, *a(gain) st the odds,* $8.00
D. Davidson / T. Mandel, *Absence Sensorium,* $14.00
Jean Day, *The I and the You,* $ 11.00
Ray DiPalma, *The Jukebox of Memnon,* $8.50
Ray DiPalma, *Provocations,* $11.00
Rachel Blau DuPlessis, *Drafts 15-XXX, The Fold,* $12.00
Rachel Blau DuPlessis, *Drafts 3-14,* $9.50
Rachel Blau DuPlessis, *Tabula Rosa,* $8.50
Theodore Enslin, *Case Book,* $8.50
Norman Fischer, *The Devices,* $7.00
Peter Ganick, *Rectangular Morning Poem,* $9.00
Michael Gottleib, *River Road,* $10.00
Jessica Grim, *Locale,* $10.00
Carla Harryman, *Vice,* $7.50
P. Inman, *Think of One,* $7.50
Andrew Levy, *Continuous Discontinuous (Curve 2),* $13.50
Sheila E. Murphy, *Falling in Love Falling in Love With You Syntax* $16.50
Susan Smith Nash, *Catfishes and Jackals,* $12.00
Melanie Neilson, *Natural Facts,* $10.50
Gil Ott, *Public Domain,* $8.50
Maureen Owen, *Untapped Maps,* $9.50
Stephen Ratcliffe, *spaces in the light said to be where one/ comes from,* $9.50
Kit Robinson, *The Champagne of Concrete,* $9.00
Leslie Scalapino, *Goya's L. A.,* $8.50
Leslie Scalapino, *How Phenomena Appear to Unfold,* $9.00
Spencer Selby, *House of Before,* 9.00
Ron Silliman, *Lit,* $7.50
Ron Silliman, *Toner,* $9.50
Diane Ward, *Imaginary Movie,* $9.50

Potes & Potes Press also publishes A.BACUS, a single-author newsletter, eight times a year; a series of Limited Editions, called Extras; POTEPOETZINE and POTEPOETTEXT, electronic texts available by free subscription to any email address by sending that email address to: potepoet@home.com; and, has some back issues of its earlier chapbook series published in 1981 and 1982.

Please write to us at:
Potes & Poets Press Inc.
181 Edgemont Avenue
Elmwood CT 06110-1005
for a complete catalogue and ordering information.